PRAISE FOR *BRAVE BUSINESS LEADERSHIP*

"*In* BRAVE Business Leadership, *General Jeff Foley makes hard truths come alive. Jeff learned bare knuckle leadership over many years in leadership positions around the world in peace and war. His insights and stories will inspire you.*"

— Lt Gen Robert L. Caslen, Jr., U.S. Army (Retired), 59th Superintendent of the United States Military Academy at West Point

"*Jeff has done a masterful job of distilling the US Army's wisdom on leadership into a highly-readable book you'll want to refer to again and again. Investing in yourself as a leader is not an option, it's imperative.*"

— Marshall Goldsmith, Thinkers 50 #1 Executive Coach for 10 years, and New York Times #1 bestselling author of Triggers, Mojo, and What Got You Here Won't Get You There

"*Jeff Foley has provided a straightforward guide for those at all levels of leadership. It is a must read for new or aspiring leaders as well as those charged with developing the next generation of competent leaders.*"

— Jerry DeMuro, CEO, BAE Systems, Inc

"*Jeff Foley's BRAVE leadership principles are desperately needed in healthcare and academic medicine. Implementing his methodology can have a dramatic impact on building leadership capacity across any organization. I particularly enjoyed seeing the many business stories that brought to life each element of BRAVE.*"

— David C. Hess, MD, Dean of the Medical College of Georgia and EVP for Medical Affairs and Integration, Augusta University

"*The BRAVE methodology is a rubric for any organization seeking to grow their generational intelligence. Jeff goes beyond simply worrying about the workplace of the future. He focuses on creating the worker of the future—*

from the inside out. If you want deeper engagement, increased loyalty and greater retention in our high-velocity and generational-shifting workplace, then BRAVE leadership is a must read."

— MICK UKLEJA, PH.D., CO-AUTHOR *MANAGING THE MILLENNIALS: DISCOVER THE CORE COMPETENCIES FOR MANAGING TODAY'S WORKFORCE* (2ND EDITION)

"Are you looking for a leadership book that will inspire you to inspire others to the highest level of leadership? This is a how-to book by a man who has been there and done that. Read this book and you will grow as a leader and never be the same again."

— JAMES H. BLANCHARD, RETIRED CHAIRMAN AND CEO, SYNOVIS FINANCIAL

"Organizational structures and technology will change over time, but Jeff reveals how leadership principals are constant. He successfully demonstrates how BRAVE principles can be applied to improve individual and group performance. This guide should be in every leader's library."

— COLONEL HERMAN E. BULLS, US ARMY (RETIRED), VICE CHAIRMAN, AMERICAS, JLL AND CORPORATE BOARD DIRECTOR

"Jeff brings out timeless principles of leadership with powerful stories from his years of military and corporate experience. Any organization looking to develop its leaders, strengthen its teams and accelerate their results will benefit from embracing the BRAVE methodology presented here."

— PAT WILLIAMS, SENIOR VICE PRESIDENT, NBA'S ORLANDO MAGIC AND AUTHOR OF *CHARACTER CARVED IN STONE*

"Jeff Foley is the authority on taking principles from the US Army and West Point and applying them to the modern business world with step-by-step clarity."

— DINA DWYER-OWENS, BRAND AMBASSADOR (FORMER CEO & CHAIR) NEIGHBORLY BRANDS, FORMER CHAIR OF THE INTERNATIONAL FRANCHISE ASSOCIATION

BRAVE BUSINESS LEADERSHIP

Grow Competent, Confident Leaders And Get Great Results

JEFFREY W. FOLEY

Brigadier General, US Army (Retired)

INDIE BOOKS
INTERNATIONAL

Additional Copyrights and Trademark References:

The Ken Blanchard Companies® and SLII® are registered trademarks of Blanchard Training and Development, Inc. (dba The Ken Blanchard Companies)

Situational Leadership® is a registered trademark of Leadership Studies, Inc.

Everything DiSC® is a registered trademark of John Wiley & Sons, Inc. All rights reserved.

Five Behaviors of a Cohesive Team® is a registered trademark of John Wiley & Sons, Inc. All rights reserved.

Marshall Goldsmith Stakeholder Centered Coaching® is a registered trademark of PRISM LTD., Guilford, United Kingdom

One Page Business Plan® is a registered trademark of the One Page Business Plan Company. All rights reserved.

ISBN-10: 1-947480-64-2
ISBN-13: 978-1-947480-64-3
Library of Congress Control Number:2019910053

Illustrations by Bill Wood

Photography by Luisa O'Connor

Designed by Joni McPherson, McPherson Graphics

INDIE BOOKS INTERNATIONAL, INC.
2424 VISTA WAY, SUITE 316
OCEANSIDE, CA 92054
www.indiebooksintl.com

This book is dedicated to my father, Albert P. Foley.

Dad was an army captain during World War II, and landed in Normandy with the US Army's Third Armored Division. He is the inspiration in my life.

Emily,
Keep leading! I'm proud of you!!

TABLE OF CONTENTS

FOREWORD

by Ken Blanchard

My father grew up in Highland Falls, New York, minutes away from the U. S. Military Academy at West Point. After high school, he went to the Naval Academy in Annapolis and ultimately retired as an admiral. I'll always hold West Point graduates in high regard based on my visits to West Point as a kid.

I've known many military leaders over the years. One great leader I'm proud to know is Brigadier General Jeff Foley—one of those West Point grads. I first met Jeff in 2010, shortly after he retired from the army. Over the years, we've become friends as I've watched him grow in his profession as a leadership coach, consultant, and speaker.

The U.S. Army is older than the United States of America. It serves as a wonderful laboratory for the study of organizational leadership. What many people don't understand is that leader development is fundamental to the army. There are no "perpetual privates"—it is either up or out. Army leaders are responsible for helping their reports become good candidates for promotion. Much can be learned from the military about the art and science of leading, and this book contributes to that effort in spades.

The depth and range of Jeff's leadership expertise is extensive. He has been successfully coaching and consulting with business leaders around the country since his retirement from the Army. His achievement in this area shows how military experience can directly contribute to business success. What's exciting for me is Jeff's desire to share the story of his growth as a leader with others who might benefit from his experience.

In this book, Jeff recounts lessons learned from his father and from other adult leaders through the Boy Scouts, competitive sports, and his four years as a cadet at West Point. These positive influences in his early life set the conditions for Jeff's successful military career.

Jeff helps readers understand the complexities of what it takes to become a competent, confident leader by sharing his own leadership practices through the *BRAVE* acronym:

- Be a leader of character
- Reveal and reinforce leader competencies
- Attack with a leader development program
- Value coaching excellence
- Embrace trusted relationships

For each element of *BRAVE*, Jeff shares an inspiring military story from his own experience and then provides a powerful story from the private sector. He demystifies military leadership as he illustrates how lessons from the army can help leaders in the business world. Jeff also provides tools leaders can put into practice immediately to develop their direct reports as well as themselves.

BRAVE will have an immediate and powerful impact on the lives of leaders at every level—from CEOs to frontline supervisors. Thanks, Jeff, for giving us the gift of your military perspective as you take us with you on your fascinating life's journey.

> Ken Blanchard
> Chief Spiritual Officer of The Ken Blanchard Companies
> Coauthor of *The One Minute Manager* and *Leading at a Higher Level*

PREFACE

Helping to develop competent, confident leaders was the task that brought me the most joy while serving a career in the United States Army. It remains a joy in my life today.

My true leadership development began with my Dad, who taught me about character and giving my best every day. It continued growing up in Cincinnati, both in the competitive sports world and in my time in the Boy Scouts of America. My development took a giant leap forward when I attended the US Military Academy at West Point, New York, (where I played center field for Army, thus the illustrations of me in a baseball uniform in this book), and spent the next thirty-two years serving in the army during peace and war.

I learned two enormously valuable lessons during my career in the army. The first was my career was guided by a long series of goals that I set. It began with graduating from the academy, then continued with every follow-on assignment. The second lesson was the realization that the richness I achieved in life was not measured in how much I received, but how much I was able to give others. When I retired from the army in 2010, I established a new goal of determining how I could best give back to others what I learned from my time in the army. I was grateful to discover the business and nonprofit worlds populated by so many people thirsting for some of what I had to offer. Thus, the second half of my life would be focused on serving others by sharing what has brought so much joy to my life.

Since 1775, the US Army has been refining its methods for creating brave leaders: competent and confident, capable of decisive action. Based on my own experiences, I became inspired to capture the essence of what I have learned into a practical, proven guide that can be immediately applied to leaders in the business world. I call the guide BRAVE. Each letter of the word BRAVE represents a key element of the guide. When applied, it can help grow leaders, grow the people being led, and ultimately produce greater results for the organization.

Would it be beneficial to have a simple, powerful, proven approach to help guide your development as a leader, and in turn help you develop your people? If so, I invite you to read on.

This book is not intended to imply endorsement from the United States Army: the lessons are based on what I learned as a proud member of the greatest army in the world.

I wish you the best in your leadership journey.

Jeffrey W. Foley
Brigadier General, US Army (Retired)

Augusta, Georgia

June 2019

SECTION I

Why Competent, Confident Leaders Matter

CHAPTER 1

Leadership Challenges In The Business World

O say does that star-spangled banner yet wave
O'er the land of the free and the home of the brave?

"THE STAR-SPANGLED BANNER" BY FRANCIS SCOTT KEY

When I reflect back on the real catalyst of my leadership development, it clearly began at Camp Red Cloud in the town of Uijeongbu, South Korea. It was July 1983. I had the privilege of being selected to command an army company of 220 soldiers. I was a captain, five years out of graduation from the United States Military Academy at West Point. My goal was simply to succeed.

The challenges were many. It was a high-risk job with a critical wartime mission thirty-five miles from the demilitarized zone separating North Korea and South Korea. I had never been in charge of so many troops with so much responsibility and authority. I had to deal with good and not-so-good bosses, causing me to rely on my own core values. I was concerned about failure. I wondered if I had all the right skills to make good decisions. Would I be an effective coach for my new lieutenants and other senior leaders? Would I be able to develop mutual trust quickly with my superiors, my team of leaders, and the soldiers? My boss was two hours away, so I was on my own in many ways and not very comfortable asking for help.

I had to recommit myself to learning about leadership. Values, leadership skills, coaching and developing others, and building trust all became monumental tasks that I had to address. Over the course of the year, I am happy to report that we achieved success. While I did not know it at the time, the BRAVE methodology for growing competence and confidence in my ability to lead was taking shape. What I also came to realize that year was the army was the right place for me.

This book is intended as a guide to help business leaders grow competence and confidence to achieve greater results. This book is not about military strategy or tactics, doctrine, or operational planning. It does not address business objectives, budget planning, or sales strategies. It is entirely about inspiring a call to action to develop leaders at all levels. Outstanding performance does not happen by accident.

The Leadership Issues Facing Businesses Today

The research is clear: CEOs and business owners today are facing enormous challenges in developing the leadership necessary to position their organizations for future success.

Development Dimensions International (DDI), a global leader in the leadership development industry, reports, "Strategy is nothing without effective leaders to execute." In a 2018 survey of 1000 C-level executives worldwide, the top two issues they face in the coming year were developing "next gen" leaders and failure to attract/retain top talent. These same two issues placed in the top five in 2016 and 2017, as well.[1]

Based on comprehensive research by the Human Capital Institute and UNC Kenan-Flagler Business School, 85 percent of organizations sur-

---

[1] Ray, Rebecca L. "For CEOs, It's Still About Developing Leaders: Strategy Is Nothing Without Effective Leaders to Execute." Development Dimensions International. 2018. Accessed February 19, 2019. https://www.ddiworld.com/DDI/media/trend-research/glf2018/global-leadership-forecast-2018_au-nz_leaders-at-the-core.pdf.

veyed agree that there is an urgent need to accelerate the development of its leaders.[2]

According to a comprehensive study by the Center for Creative Leadership, the top leadership challenges facing organizations around the world include:

1. **Developing managerial effectiveness** is the challenge of developing the relevant skills—such as time management, prioritization, strategic thinking, decision-making, and getting up to speed with the job—to be more effective at work.

2. **Inspiring others** is the challenge of inspiring or motivating others to ensure they're satisfied with their jobs and working smarter.

3. **Developing employees** is the challenge of developing others, including mentoring and coaching.

4. **Leading a team** is the challenge of team-building, team development, and team management. Specific challenges include how to instill pride, how to provide support, how to lead a big team, and what to do when taking over a new team.[3]

The environment in which business leaders find themselves today continues to evolve, especially in the world of technology. Change happens faster, information is more available than ever, and transparency is the norm. Competition is tough in just about every industry. Some pains remain at the top of many lists: inability to attract and retain top talent, lack of accountability, lack of courage to make tough decisions,

[2] Human Capital Institute. "How to Accelerate Leadership Development." UNC Kenan-Flagler Business School. 2014. Accessed February 19, 2019. https://www.kenan-flagler.unc.edu/~/media/Files/documents/executive-development/unc-webcast-accelerate-leadership-development-deck.pdf.

[3] "The Top 6 Leadership Challenges Around the World." Center for Creative Leadership, 2017. Accessed February 19, 2019. https://www.ccl.org/articles/leading-effectively-articles/top-6-leadership-challenges/.

lack of employee engagement, unethical and inappropriate conduct, and lack of trust. Vast knowledge and experience will disappear when the baby boomers begin retiring in large numbers in the coming years.

Many corporate leaders also perpetuate a profit-first mentality that often trumps focused efforts to develop other leaders. Measuring what results are achieved is clearly a critical task, but measuring how those results are achieved cannot be ignored.

According to Gallup studies, over the past twenty years, employee engagement has been one of the most important factors affecting profitability, productivity, quality, turnover, and safety. Bad managers cost business billions of dollars every year, their research shows. Managers who have the knowledge, experience, and skills to be effective makes a significant difference in achieving an engaged workforce. Specifically, Gallup concludes that great managers possess five talents:

1. They motivate every single employee to take action, and they engage employees with a compelling mission and vision.

2. They have the assertiveness to drive outcomes and the ability to overcome adversity and resistance.

3. They create a culture of clear accountability.

4. They build relationships that create trust, open dialogue, and full transparency.

5. They make decisions based on productivity, not politics.[4]

The best executives and business leaders want to achieve sustained, long-term success. They want to maintain a reputation of providing quality products and services as well as to be good partners in the communities they serve. They want to reward their shareholders and stakeholders. These traits are no different than those of leaders in the army.

---

[4] Beck, Randall, and Jim Harter. "Why Great Managers Are So Rare." Gallup.com, March 25, 2014. Accessed February 22, 2019. https://news.gallup.com/businessjournal/167975/why-great-managers-rare. aspx.

The requirement for trust between leaders and their people remains one of the most important priorities for corporate leaders. Establishing a culture of learning centered around core values that drive behaviors is of paramount importance to establishing mutual trust. The need to develop people in their ability to lead, to build bench strength, to identify high-potential performers, and to increase levels of individual and team performance are all important.

There are huge gaps, however, in the business world when it comes to developing leaders. In many highly technical fields like health care and engineering, leadership is often omitted entirely in the curriculum of study and preparation. According to research by Zenger Folkman, the average leader in the business world does not receive leadership training until ten years *after* they first began supervising others.[5] Another study by CEB (Gartner) Learning and Development Roundtable highlighted that 60 percent of frontline managers underperform during the first two years.[6] These two data points are interesting and *discouraging*.

The Generation Discussion

Some fundamental leadership competencies never become obsolete. They have been constants in the army and business world. They are generation-independent. That is why some leadership books remain perennial bestsellers. Examples of these fundamentals include the need to build trust, to inspire, to hold people accountable, and to become good decision makers. With the growth of the millennial generation and their successors, these fundamentals will remain constant. What needs to evolve, however, is how best to achieve and implement these qualities. That is why understanding generational differences is important.

---

[5] Zenger, Jack. "Are You Starting Too Late? A Head Start on the Path to Extraordinary." ZengerFolkman. com. Accessed 2014. http://zengerfolkman.com/wp-content/uploads/2013/03/Leadership-Development-Are-You-Starting-Too-Late.pdf.

[6] Thorn, Chantal. "3 (Not So Secret) Secrets to Designing Effective Leadership Development Programs." D2L.com. Accessed 2017. https://www.d2l.com/enterprise/blog/3-not-secret-secrets-designing-effective-leadership-development-programs/

Millennials are the most knowledgeable of all generations. In the book *Managing the Millennials*, the authors conclude the millennial generation of people work, think, and set priorities differently than previous generations.[7] They also have a different set of intrinsic values: work-life balance, reward, self-expression, attention, achievement, informality, simplicity, multitasking, and meaning. Leaders who want to attract and retain millennials must be aware of these intrinsic values.

A common trend in today's workforce is frequent moving from job to job, without loyalty to any particular company. Without a proven method to attract and develop leaders, the current nomadic nature of the workforce will wreak havoc on organizations.

A survey of millennials merits consideration as well. In 2016, Deloitte surveyed over 7,000 millennials from twenty-nine countries about their views on and experiences in the workforce. Seventy-one percent of those likely to leave their current jobs in the next two years reported being unhappy with how their leadership skills were being developed. Those likely to remain longest in their current position shared their organization's values, were more satisfied with a sense of purpose beyond financial success, reported that use was made of their skills, and said their professional development was a priority. Millennials in senior management would prefer a greater sense of purpose around "being the best possible place to work."[8]

One keen insight into how businesses maximize human potential is highlighted by the annual "Great Places to Work" survey published by *Fortune* magazine. Companies are measured on executive team effec-

---

[7] Espinoza, Chip, and Mick Ukleja. *Managing the Millennials: Discover the Core Competencies for Managing Today's Workforce*. John Wiley & Sons, Inc., 2016.

[8] Deloitte Touche Tohmatsu Limited. "The 2016 Deloitte Millennial Survey: Winning Over the Next Generation of Leaders." Deloitte.com. Accessed February 21, 2019. https://www2.deloitte.com/content/dam/Deloitte/global/Documents/About-Deloitte/gx-millenial-survey-2016-exec-summary.pdf.

tiveness, innovation, people-focused programs, level of trust, credible and respectful leadership, pride in the work, and camaraderie.[9]

The Birth Of The BRAVE Methodology

Upon graduation from West Point, I was assigned as a platoon leader, responsible for the training and welfare of fifty soldiers, twenty-five vehicles, and several millions of dollars in communications systems. Over the next thirty years, I progressed through the ranks up to the executive level of the army. Each assignment carried increased responsibilities over all aspects of running an organization, to include but not limited to personnel systems and accountability, intelligence and security, training, operations, planning, maintenance, logistics, and managing the budget. I found that I had to recommit myself to the army and update my focused goals for each assignment. While my time as a captain at Camp Red Cloud served as the real catalyst for my growth, every year of my service built upon that experience.

My guide is based on the word BRAVE, derived from my thirty-two years of experience in the army. Each letter of the word BRAVE represents a key element of what I believe it takes to become a competent, confident leader. BRAVE serves as a roadmap for those genuinely interested in growing themselves and the people they lead. It is summarized below, with discussion and stories highlighting the implementation of each element throughout the rest of the book.

- **Be** a leader of character
- **R**eveal and reinforce leader competencies
- **A**ttack with a leader development program
- **V**alue coaching excellence
- **E**mbrace trusted relationships

---

[9] "100 Best Companies to Work For." Fortune. Accessed December 11, 2018. http://fortune.com/best-companies/.

Summary

The US Army, founded on June 14, 1775, is older than the United States. It is one of our nation's longest-running organizations. It also serves as a fascinating laboratory in the study of organizational leadership. While the army provides a powerful leadership development process, the burden of execution rests with leaders at all levels to serve their people. Military leaders must be committed to continuous learning themselves and effective coaching of others to maximize the growth of their people.

Once you have been on a high-performing team, you never lose your hunger for it. The BRAVE approach is designed to help you get there.

Why BRAVE? Francis Scott Key is the author of the famous words "the land of the free and the home of the brave." He wrote those words in 1814, and since 1931, they have been sung as the national anthem of the United States. The army and its sister services, since their birth, have distinguished themselves through filling their ranks with brave men and women. Being a great leader takes courage. It takes bravery. The word *brave* also highlights the warrior ethos: the special spirit of being a soldier.

In the next chapter, BRAVE is introduced with a compelling story of how it impacted one business leader. Section II of this book shares a comprehensive description of the BRAVE methodology. Section III covers how the BRAVE methodology can contribute to building your organizational culture.

Sharing the BRAVE methodology to help develop leaders has become my life's work.

How Best To Use This Book

This book is intended as a guide to help business leaders grow themselves and become more effective in creating high-performing organizations. It is a call to action. To get the most out of this book:

- Commit to becoming the best leader you can be—get your head in the game.

- Read the entire book first, including the appendices, to get a good feel for the significant challenges facing business leaders and the solutions offered.

- Reread each of the BRAVE chapters with a focus on the Leadership Tips at the end of each chapter, which serve as a guide to how to achieve success.

- Perform an individual assessment of your state of development based on BRAVE, found in Appendix A.

- Based on your assessment, develop a personal action plan that identifies with precision what you will do, when you will complete it, and what assistance or resources are needed for success.

- Assess your performance based on your action plan and modify your actions accordingly.

- Review this book periodically to get refreshed and re-inspired.

- Find time for quiet reflection on your leadership journey and on how the BRAVE guide can best serve you and your leadership team.

Enjoy your journey.

CHAPTER 2

The BRAVE Methodology

The US Army has a history of growing competent and confident leaders like the brave soldiers who led the defense of Fort McHenry during the War of 1812, the inspiration for our national anthem. That army legacy of leaders with character is the inspiration for this book. The pursuit of building character began with the creation of our army in 1775 and has never stopped.

Step back in time to August 3, 1776; the place is Long Island, New York. Just one month after the signing of the Declaration of Independence, US Army Commander in Chief General George Washington is preparing for an imminent attack by superior forces led by British General William Howe. Washington knows his army. They are common laborers, smiths, and farmhands. They are outmanned and outgunned. He has to turn these undisciplined soldiers into a warrior-class force with a sharp edge to cut through the bonds of colonial attachment to England. Character is on Washington's mind. He needs leaders. He needs men who are going to inspire the troops. How is he going to build this army, particularly the officer leadership, who will have the sustained strength and tenacity to defeat this monumental foe? One important step he takes is issuing this general order:

August 3, 1776

The General is sorry to be informed that the foolish and wicked practice of profane cursing and swearing, a vice hitherto little known in our American Army is growing into fashion. He hopes that the officers will, by example as well as influence, endeavor to check it and that both they and the men will reflect that we can little hope of the blessing of Heaven on our army if we insult it by our impiety and folly. Added to this it is a vice so mean and low without any temptation that every man of sense and character detests and despises it.

(Signed,) George Washington[10]

Fast forward to the height of the Civil War and another leadership milestone. In a world that held all is fair in war, President and Commander in Chief Abraham Lincoln, in April of 1863, takes a brave step by signing guidelines called the Lieber Code, dictating how soldiers should conduct themselves with character in wartime. The Lieber Code is sometimes referred to as the first modern codification of the laws of war.[11] Named after its main author, law professor Francis Lieber, the Code regulates a variety of issues, in particular, the interplay between military necessity and the treatment of civilians and prisoners.

Preserving the Union was of utmost importance to President Lincoln; equally important was establishing quality leaders of the nation's armed forces.

It was the summer of 2010, and I was retiring from the army. Thirty-two years had passed since graduation from West Point. I had the privilege to serve all over the world, in constantly changing environments, in peace and war. As it had been for so many before me, it was going to be a bittersweet day.

---

[10] "Washington's Order Against Profanity." Ushistory.org, Independence Hall Association, Accessed February 21, 2019 http://www.ushistory.org/valleyforge/washington/profanity.html.

[11] Labuda, Patryk I. "Lieber Code." Oxford Public International Law. September 2014. Accessed June 7, 2017. opil.ouplaw.com/view/10.1093/law:epil/9780199231690/law-9780199231690-e2126

What I loved most about the army was the opportunity to develop leaders. How effective I was at this task is up to others to judge, but I know I was committed to that task from day one.

How was I going to capitalize on that passion in my game plan for the next phase of my life? How could I best capture my experience as a leader and coach to help business leaders who may not have had the vast opportunities to learn like I was blessed with from my time in the army? What were the most transferable skills I learned from leading military organizations ranging in size from forty to 8000 people that could be of significant value to corporate America?

Over the past eight years, I have conducted presentations and workshops for leaders across the country for a wide variety of organizations. I have met some magnificent people who were enormously successful leading organizations of all sizes. In my travels, I was also very encouraged by the business community embracing the lessons I shared on leadership from the army.

In 2012, I had the opportunity to meet Dr. Ken Blanchard when I was invited to become a trustee for a global nonprofit company he cofounded that focused on leadership in the faith-based world. Over the years, Ken became an important mentor in my life. He helped me gain a much deeper and richer understanding of all aspects of leadership, especially connecting with the business world. He inspired me in many ways to achieve success in my new leadership consulting and coaching profession.

Understanding The Military Environment

There are no guarantees of success for any approach to developing great leaders. But the US Army has been at this task since June 14, 1775, when it was formed by the Continental Congress. Some powerful, proven methods have emerged that can help you develop yourself and your team.

The number of CEOs who got their start in the military has decreased over the years but remains significant.[12] Studies show CEOs who have military experience are 60 percent less likely to commit fraud than other CEOs and lead their organizations more successfully during economic downturns. Those CEOs with military experience also bring a focus on ethical principles to the C-suite that other CEOs may lack.[13]

When the US Army became an all-volunteer force in 1973, along with all the military services, it became a real competitor with American businesses. Military leaders suffered many of the same pains business leaders suffer from (highlighted previously). The army has also taken action over many decades to address each of them; that work continues.

When I deliver presentations to the corporate world, I am often asked what the similarities are between the army and business. Let me highlight some facts about the military that can help you discover real benefits to your organization.

The military is an up-or-out organization. You either get promoted, or you are gone. There are no lifetime privates or lieutenants. The succession strategy consists of every leader throughout the organization being responsible for developing subordinates for future promotion. This tremendous focus on helping subordinates develop is one key element of the servant-leadership culture in the military. Comprehensive, two-page performance assessments on every soldier, from sergeant to general, are an integral part of the army culture, providing the foundation on which promotions and selections for critical leadership positions are based.

---

[12] "Do CEOs with Military Experience Outperform Others?" ChiefExecutive.net. May 31, 2012. Accessed June 16, 2017. https://chiefexecutive.net/do-ceos-with-military-experience-outperform-others__trashed/.

[13] Fisman, Ray. "CEOs Who Served in the Military Are More Honest. But They Make Their Companies Less Money." Slate Magazine. May 25, 2012. Accessed December 11, 2018. https://slate.com/business/2012/05/ceos-who-served-in-the-military-are-they-more-honest.html.

Military organizations are highly structured out of necessity, primarily along functional lines. This structure establishes lines of responsibility and authority, clarifying who does what. Disciplined decision-making is enhanced, especially in crisis situations. More effective communication, more efficient use and dissemination of resources, and focused training are all enabled by this structure. Combined with the structure are well-established processes documented in manuals, policies, and standard operating procedures.

Tremendous responsibilities are assigned to sergeants and officers at a young age. As an example, brand new lieutenants fresh out of West Point or the Reserve Officers' Training Corps (ROTC) are immediately put into leadership positions and held accountable for forty to seventy-five people, millions of dollars of equipment, and accomplishing their wartime mission. Responsibilities increase incrementally as soldiers are promoted.

The army has adapted how it trains soldiers over the years to accommodate every generation of new soldiers. Wherever possible, technology and other social aspects are integrated into the environment. By the same token, however, many leadership skills and techniques used to inspire and develop soldiers *don't* change, as they are timeless. The military invests heavily in educating soldiers to *think* and training them to *act*. Education and training occur in schools and in military units throughout the army.

For many folks not in the military, a common misperception merits explanation. The myth is that productivity only comes from the strict, hierarchical command-and-control leadership exercised daily by those with the highest rank. There is some truth to that, especially during times of crisis, when quick decisions need to be made or when the risks are too high for delegation. The vast majority of the time, however, when life is not on the line, nothing could be farther from the truth. The army depends heavily on knowledge, skills, and experiences of leaders at all levels. To maximize agility on the battlefield and the ability to adapt to rapidly changing conditions effectively, delegation of authority and responsibility to the lowest level possible is the goal.

The above characterization of the United States military highlights lessons learned over almost two-and-a-half centuries. Many of the threads of this success have become part of the American business culture. The military has been enormously successful for many decades at developing leaders. The real proof of the US Army's leader development program's effectiveness is the fact that the US Army is one of the best-trained and led armies in the world. This book highlights key aspects of military leader development that can have a direct and positive impact on you and your organization, regardless of size.

The Army Investment In Training Leaders

The army is made up of men and women who voluntarily take an oath to serve: "I do solemnly swear (or affirm) that I will support and defend the Constitution of the United States against all enemies, foreign and domestic; that I will bear true faith and allegiance to the same."[14]

Recruits come from all walks of life, all races, all religious faiths, creeds, and generations. Men and women enlist to serve from two to six years and have the opportunity to reenlist (sign up for an additional tour of duty) upon the end of their initial contract. Everyone attends basic training as their cultural indoctrination into the military. Officers are commissioned when they graduate from the US Military Academy or other universities via the ROTC program; a smaller percentage of officers come from Officer Candidate School (OCS) after completing basic training as enlisted soldiers. Officers are obligated to serve for designated periods based on their initial contracts.

---

[14] "Oath of Enlistment". US Army. https://www.army.mil/e2/downloads/rv7/values/posters/enlistment.pdf

The US Army selects hundreds of officers to lead battalions (300–1,000 people), brigades (2,000–5,000 people), and divisions (10,000–20,000 people) every year. These positions are similar to executive roles in the business world, in which CEO/presidents are responsible for all aspects of running effective, efficient organizations focused on accomplishing the mission. Business leaders stand to learn much from the army about how to lead organizations of all sizes.

To be successful in the US Army, you must have an intense desire to learn your technical profession *and* how to deal with people. Soldiers progress through the ranks via performance-based promotions, earning positions of increased responsibility. Building competent and confident leaders at all levels, from the executive team down to first-line supervisors, is a perpetual goal.

Mission failure is not acceptable in the army. To maximize the potential for success, the army grows its own leaders. The fundamentals of how the army grows its own are documented in what is called a field manual: *Field Manual 22-100 Army Leadership* (1999), later revised in *Field Manual 6-22 Army Leadership* (2006).[15, 16] These manuals are among the best produced by the army, in my opinion, and are updated regularly.

Field Manual 6-22 Army Leadership captures the essence of the army's approach to developing leaders:

> *Leader development is fundamental to our Army—leader development is the deliberate, continuous, sequential, and progressive process—founded in Army values—that grows Soldiers and Army Civilians into competent and confident leaders capable of decisive action. Leader development is achieved through the life-long synthesis of the knowledge,*

---

[15] *U. S. Army Field Manual 22-100*, Army Leadership, Headquarters, Dept of the Army, 1999.

[16] *U. S. Army Field Manual 6-22*: Army Leadership. Headquarters, Dept. of the Army, 2006.

skills, and experiences gained through the training and education opportunities in the institutional, operational, and self-development domains.

The army recognized long ago that learning to lead is a journey, from knowing yourself to building one-on-one relationships and leading teams. The need to keep learning never ends.

One of the most vital reasons why the US Army has sustained tremendous success over decades is its relentless focus on the development of its leaders. Great leaders know not only how to survive today, but also how to win in the future, whether on the battlefield or in the corporate marketplace.

My BRAVE Methodology

BRAVE offers a proven methodology that can help grow competence and confidence in your ability to lead and help those in your organization do the same.

Leadership is a tough business. To be good at leadership demands commitment and sacrifice like few other tasks in life. Everyone, regardless of title or position, can lead through influencing others. But leading organizations, especially large ones, is not in everybody's wheelhouse.

There is an art and science to becoming an effective leader. The art focuses on how we connect, how we inspire, how we touch the hearts and souls of those we lead. The science addresses more measurable skills, like clarifying goals and effective delegation of tasks. Some people do enter this world with a more refined aptitude for leading, but the best leaders are those who are in tireless pursuit of learning.

You have a choice to make about your growth as a leader. You first must commit yourself to that goal. BRAVE is a straightforward, practical, holistic approach that can help you grow as a leader and make better leaders of your people. This approach is not a fad or a trend. It is fundamentally based on how the army enables the development of its leaders; it has stood the test of time. While common sense comes to mind with each of these elements, it will take discipline to make them a common practice in your behavior and those in your organization. The focus here is to train our minds so that our behaviors are consistent with our values, and hence become instinctual. BRAVE leaders are key and essential in building high-performing organizations.

The five most powerful lessons I learned about leadership during my career in the army make up the components of BRAVE.

- **B:** *Be a leader of character.* Character is at the heart of being an effective leader. It represents who we are and what we stand for. No amount of leadership competency can overcome a lack of character. Character begins with a comprehensive understanding of oneself, a necessary condition before people can effectively understand others. Character is fundamentally defined by those values or deep beliefs that guide behavior every day of our lives, on and off duty. Leaders of character define and communicate those values to earn the trust and confidence of their followers. They bring values to life through living them, holding others accountable for living them, and rewarding others who live them as well.

- **R:** *Reveal and reinforce leader competencies.* Clearly documented fundamental leadership competencies make clear what is most important to leaders in an organization. They define success. Uncover them. Bring them to life. Core competencies highlight what it takes to be an effective member of a team. As one progresses up through the organization, additional leadership skills, commensurate with a leader's level of responsibility, also must be identified.

At the executive level, the environment is characterized by increased complexity, higher risk, greater uncertainty, and less direct control over subordinate echelons. There is a risk to any organization if competencies remain hidden or are left up to chance. Clearly document them in employee handbooks, integrate them into the performance appraisal system, and reinforce them during regular scheduled check-ins and coaching sessions.

- *A: Attack with a leader development program.* The best leaders take action to develop themselves and their people. Good development programs focused on the needs of the organization help prepare current and future leaders to lead their teams. Good programs attract and retain the best talent and set the conditions for the organization's success. Once developed, rigorous execution of the program is paramount. Recognize the importance of sustained investment in the development of people. Business leaders own the task of developing their people and cannot ignore it.

- *V: Value coaching excellence.* Effective one-on-one coaching is a critical skill that great leaders possess. Effective coaching inspires in others an internal drive to act ethically, without direction, to achieve goals. Effective coaching drives performance and builds competence as well as confidence. Effective coaching also requires you to believe in yourself. You must believe that you can have an impact in the workplace and that you can inspire others to achieve goals they might not otherwise achieve. The real question is not *if* you will make a difference, but *what* difference you will make. Establishing a disciplined approach to the coaching sessions, identifying goals, and enforcing accountability by assessing performance are all important skills to master.

- **E: Embrace trusted relationships.** Trusted relationships between leaders and their people trumps *everything* when it comes to effective leadership. A leader's influence over others will not manifest if mutual trust is absent. Trust starts with a leader who has integrity and believes in the core values of the organization. Additional factors that drive trust include being competent in technical and leadership skills, genuinely caring for people, and possessing a sense of humility. Spending quality time with your people outside the normal work environment can be a great enabler of trust as it helps break down communication barriers. In the military, soldiers will follow their leaders into the most dangerous places, under the most extraordinary conditions, if they trust their leaders. In the business world, people will enthusiastically embrace the most challenging tasks, under conditions of chaos or uncertainty, if they trust their leaders.

✮ A BRAVE Success Story ✮

William The New President

William leaned back in his chair in his windowless office, staring at his computer monitor, trying to concentrate on a crisis that was brewing in the company. His mind was elsewhere, for he had a huge problem of his own.

Let me take you back three years. For twenty years, William had been a seasoned professional in the home improvement business. He had progressed through the ranks steadily, earning the respect and trust of his peers. Then the CEO promoted him to general manager of the flagship store. It was the biggest of five stores, and the CEO considered William to be his top performer. William was happily married and had three great children. Life was good.

Over the next three years, he watched the CEO acquire seven more stores across three additional states with gross revenue of more than $45 million. William knew the organization was ill-prepared for the rapid expansion. The CEO knew it too, but the opportunities for growth were too good to pass up. The CEO created a new position of president and appointed William to that role.

Until that moment, William had never felt fear.

Life had changed.

William felt confident that he was best qualified for the new position, but he had no real idea of how he was going to succeed. He had no experience even *working* in a company as big as the company had grown, let alone leading it. It was also not clear to him what his exact roles and authorities were as president. The challenges were enormous, from gaps in organizational structure and processes to a multitude of individual store cultures. Leadership challenges existed throughout the new enterprise. All eyes were on him. Expectations were sky high. He had a deep, sinking feeling that the organization had entered stormy seas that were only going to get more treacherous. He saw himself in the image of the Greek Titan, Atlas, holding up the globe.

William was in the toughest position of his life. But make no mistake—he had his head in the game and was fully committed to be the best president he could be.

The good news is the CEO was absolutely committed to ensuring William's success. In multiple discussions, they agreed it was time to hire me, a former army general officer, as William's coach.

William established clear goals for this effort. He wanted to increase his level of confidence and competence to perform as president of the company. He wanted to improve those leadership competencies that were essential to his success. He wanted to improve his ability to make the many changes necessary to build the foundation to sustain the company for long-term success. He had to grow the culture of the organization around a set of core values. He had to increase the effectiveness of the senior leadership team and ensure all were aligned on the vision for the future.

While William was hungry to learn and looking forward to working with me, he was skeptical as to whether I was going to provide what he needed to be successful. He had great respect for those who had served in the military, but he had never worn the uniform. He was wrestling with preconceived notions about how the army operated very differently than his company. He knew the army was a hierarchical, command-and-control organization, quite different from his company. He believed army success was based largely on a disciplined force of soldiers who knew how to follow orders. In his mind, the army did not have customers to please, nor did it have to make a financial profit. These were distinct differences from his company.

Through multiple conversations, I was able to dispel many of the myths about how the army operates. I highlighted similarities between the army and his company. He became enthused about what he could learn from my experience leading army units from forty to 8,000 people. He began to appreciate how the fundamentals that make the army so successful would be very appealing to his company. Some of these key elements included the focus on a values-based culture, leader development, effective organizational structures, disciplined operations, enforced accountability, and building teams that worked well together.

William also had never hired a coach in his professional life. But through his extensive participation in competitive athletics growing up, he valued what good coaches could bring. If he could harness what the general had to offer, there would a great benefit to him as president and to the organization as a whole.

Thus began our coaching partnership.

I started meeting with William every two weeks with a focus initially on making positive and lasting change in his leadership behaviors, then expanding the experience to discover other significant challenges that needed to be addressed.

William's level of frustration began to increase as he realized the more he learned about himself and what the company needed, the more he needed to learn. He began spending much more time in the office in the evenings and on weekends, which was taking an additional toll on his family. He was also still the CEO's go-to guy to put out fires around the company, which were many.

William remain fully engaged in pursuit of his goals. His frustration gradually transitioned to excitement about the knowledge he was gaining in his role as president and the progress the company was making as well.

Eighteen months later, a number of significant results were achieved. William had increased his level of competence and confidence in his role as president. He had developed a strategy to build and sustain a values-based culture (*Be* a leader of character). Through comprehensive leadership behavior assessments, he had learned the most important shortfalls in his leadership competencies (*Reveal* and reinforce leader competencies). He had developed a series of action plans to address his own leadership growth and to meet the goals of his organization, from senior leadership to other key positions throughout the organization (*Attack* with a development program). He had invested significant time in his own ability to coach others and helped guide the leadership team in raising the bar on their own coaching abilities (*Value* coaching excellence). William's tireless and transparent effort to focus on becoming a better leader, along with his existing genuine care for his people, helped him increase the level of mutual trust with his people (*Embrace* trusted relationships).

Today, the company is on glide path to achieve record levels of success for the year, with the prognosis for the future even brighter. William's fear gradually evolved into competence and confidence in his role as president. His work is far from complete. The journey continues.

The Path Forward

In section two, the BRAVE approach will be described in detail. Each chapter is focused on one element and will include an important reference to the US Army. Military stories, as well as corporate stories, will reinforce the key takeaways that enabled positive and lasting growth in leader performance.

Three Primary Reasons Why Business Leaders Should Consider BRAVE

- BRAVE is a straightforward, practical guide to help grow effectiveness as a leader.

- The advantage it brings is that it is fundamentally based on proven techniques used for decades by the US Army.

- When applied, it can help grow leaders, grow the people being led, and ultimately produce greater results for the business.

SECTION II

How To Build BRAVE Leaders

CHAPTER 3

Be A Leader Of Character

Bottom Line Up Front: *To be a leader of character you must discover yourself, establish and communicate core values, and live the values.*

Being a leader of character is fundamental to knowing who you are and what you stand for.

Leaders of character are honest. They do what they say they are going to do. They follow a code of ethics: those established rules of conduct that all are expected to obey. They have a passion for doing what is right and accepting the consequences of their actions. They stand up for causes they believe in. They are not afraid to admit mistakes. They believe in loyalty to themselves, their families, and their work. They have the courage to hold themselves accountable for failures in their organization. They show that they have a heart by exercising humility and empathy. They show tough love when the situation calls for it. They are selfless in their service to others. In short, they do not simply talk the talk; they walk it. They are good role models.

Becoming known as a leader of character based on trust takes time, often years. The foundation for trust, however, can be fragile. Trust can be destroyed by one bad decision, behavior, or action. Therein lies the need to recognize that being a leader of character is an everyday, all-day responsibility.

To this day, I am thankful I received a congressional nomination to West Point in 1974. Arriving there was one of the most exciting—and scary—days of my life. I signed in to basic cadet training, was issued uniforms, and life at the academy commenced.

My character-building began on day one at the academy when we all took an oath of enlistment as new cadets: "I do solemnly swear (or affirm) that I will support and defend the Constitution of the United States against all enemies, foreign and domestic; that I will bear true faith and allegiance to the same."

Character development is so critical to the army officer corps, the actual mission statement of the US Military Academy includes the words: "Educate, train, and inspire the Corps of Cadets so that each graduate is a commissioned leader of character committed to the values of Duty, Honor, Country and prepared for a career of professional excellence and service to the Nation as an officer in the United States Army."[17]

It very quickly became clear to each new cadet that serving in our army was not about us. It is about something far greater: our nation and our comrades.

The academy has an honor code that is at the foundation of building leaders of character: "*I will not lie, cheat, or steal, nor tolerate those who do.*" Leadership development goes beyond this code alone and is incorporated into every aspect of life at the academy: military, physical, and academic programs. In the May 2015 *West Point Leader Development System Handbook*, then superintendent, Lieutenant General Robert L. Caslen, highlighted in his guidance to the Corps, "*To lead soldiers and units effectively…graduates need a strong foundation of values-based leadership skills.*"[18] I suspect nowhere in our country, or the world for

---

[17] The U.S. Military Academy at West Point. https://westpoint.edu/about/SitePages/Mission.aspx Mission.

[18] *West Point Leader Development System Handbook.* Author's copy, 2015. PDF.

that matter, are values of an academic institution more relevant and enforced than the US Military Academy.

Another key distinction about the academy is the vast majority of professors and cadre are army officers. Most of them hold master's degrees with recent experience in the army. They are typically only ten to twelve years older than the cadets. These officers become wonderful character role models sharing real-life army experiences with the cadets. This is in sharp contrast to most universities, where PhDs are the rule, many of whom are much older than the students and have never served in the organizations in which graduates are destined to work.

Values-based living, the honor code, and the focus on character development were not a hard transition for me. My father had the biggest influence on my life. I was also well taught and led by my teachers, coaches, and my experiences in the Boy Scouts.

Over the years, incidents occurred that violated the trust our nation had in its army and adversely impacted the effectiveness of the force itself. In the mid-1990s, Army Chief of Staff General Dennis Reimer initiated the Character Development XXI program to address continuing challenges within the force as well as to look ahead to the future requirements of army leaders in the twenty-first century.[19]

I will never forget what emerged from that Character Development XXI effort—principally, the formal establishment of seven values. While the army has had for many years an ethical code, values, and principles, this set of new values took on a life of its own, in a big way. These values form the foundation for military character development that remains intact today. The seven values identified were loyalty, duty, respect, selfless service, honor, integrity, and personal courage

---

[19] Reimer, Dennis J. and James Jay Carafano. "Soldiers Are Our Credentials: The Collected Works and Selected Papers of the Thirty-Third Chief of Staff, United States Army." CMH Publications, 2000. Accessed February 24, 2019. https://history.army.mil/html/books/070/70-69-1/index.html.

(see Appendix C). Along with the seven values, processes were put into place to ensure leaders taught them, lived them, and were tasked with making values and character-building an integral part of everyday decision-making.

To help communicate the priority of values in the force, General Reimer communicated this personal memo to all generals, sent May 14, 1997:

> *Values are at the core of everything the army is and does. The army is more than an organization—it is an institution of people with unique and enduring values. ...The terms we use to articulate our values—duty, integrity, loyalty, selfless service, courage, respect, and honor—inspire the sense of purpose necessary to sustain our soldiers in combat and help resolve the ambiguities of military operations short of war. Leaders of character and competence live these values. We must build and maintain an army where people do what is right, where we treat each other as we would want to be treated, and where everyone can truly be all they can be.[20]*

The seven values were rolled out with a grand strategy to inform and update the entire force. Manuals and training programs were revised to increase clarity of expectations regarding behavior. What really got the attention of all was their inclusion on the first page of the performance appraisals of every soldier, from sergeant to general. The supervisor was required to assess whether the soldier demonstrated living each value with a simple "Yes" or "No." Needless to say, "No" responses for any value would be potentially career-ending for soldiers. The intent, of course, was to encourage periodic reviews with subordinates where discussions on values would take place, ultimately to eliminate the potential for a "No" assessment.

---

[20] Ibid.

One key lesson to be learned here is that values definition and enforcement must start at the top of the organization.

Bob McDonald was then chief operating officer (later chairman, president, and CEO) of one of the largest companies in the world, the Procter and Gamble Company. As the COO, he would routinely speak to new hires and students at American universities about his company. In my communication with Bob, he shared with me that he would talk about values during these presentations, citing that the best companies and leaders operate by a clear purpose and consistent set of principles and values. He truly believed that people like working for leaders who are transparent about what's important to them.

Character is who you are, how you act, and what you stand for. Reputation is how others perceive you. Both are at stake every day.

Three important tasks can help you improve your ability to lead with character.

Discover Yourself

In August 2012, I had the great pleasure of meeting Bob Buford. Buford was an author, a prominent business executive, and a long-time mentee of Peter Drucker. We were in Chicago attending the annual meeting for a global nonprofit company for which we were both trustees. After dinner, I spent forty-five memorable minutes with Buford talking about leadership, his wonderful book *Halftime*, my passion for developing leaders, and seeking significance in the second half of life. The notes I took on insights he shared with me filled the margins of the that evening's special dinner menu I took off the table. One of the most powerful lessons he shared was the need for me to lead myself before I could effectively lead others. I kind of knew that, but he drove it home. I had to refocus on the understanding of who I am, what my strengths were, what I enjoyed doing, what I am *not* good at, and what deep beliefs that reside in my heart that drive how I live my life.

Being a competent and confident leader requires self-awareness. Most people have a better idea of what they are not good at doing compared to understanding what they do well. Credible leaders need to have a realistic understanding of who they are to avoid becoming ineffective, arrogant, or irrelevant.

You are really *five* people:

- Who you think you are,

- Who your subordinates think you are,

- Who your peers think you are,

- Who your manager thinks you are,

- The real you.

How others see you is often at odds with how you *think* you are. And chances are, you are not as brilliant, decisive, communicative, or charismatic as you sometimes think.

You must also understand your strengths, what you are good at, and what you enjoy doing. Why? Because leaders are most effective when they are doing what they like to do. You need to know what motivates you and what challenges you. You need to know your behavior tendencies in normal and stressful situations. You need to know what is important in your life, what you care about. You need to know how you learn and how you make decisions. You should ask yourself the question: Are you a serving or a self-serving leader? Before you can help others discover their answers to these questions, you must lead yourself.

Another critical element of self-awareness is understanding how others perceive you. There is tremendous value in learning from feedback from those you work with, including managers, peers, and direct reports. Effective research-based tools can help guide that process. Also, if you are able to let go of your ego, you can learn by asking people for feedback on specific leadership skills. This knowledge helps expose your blind spots: things others know about you, but which you may not know about yourself.

One very effective way to learn about you and learn how others perceive you is through research-based assessments. Millions of people take behavior assessments every year. I have taken many in the army and after retirement and each one helped me gain a better understanding of myself. When used effectively they help people learn their own behavioral tendencies, what they like doing, what motivates them, and expose blind spots through feedback from others.

Establish And Communicate Core Values

Lots of things change in organizations: products, services, technology, and competition. Values are the exception. Values do not change overnight. They are forged in one's heart and soul over time, beginning in our youth. Parents, siblings, relatives, peers, teachers, coaches, scout leaders, pastors, priests, rabbis, and Sunday school teachers all are influencers. As we age, the influencers expand to include managers and colleagues at work, elected officials, historical figures, friends, children…the list goes on.

If you ever spent time in the Boy Scouts of America, you will appreciate how that experience helped shape the character of young men. Earning Eagle Scout remains one of my fondest achievements as a youth. Scouting was where I first actually saw values in writing, was required to memorize them, and learned over time the expected behaviors associated with each. Understanding and living the Scout Oath and Scout Law (see Appendix B) helped prepare me for success at West Point, in the army, and in life. That was because I learned what these values meant, how to internalize them, and got motivated to live them when I saw other great leaders do the same.

Unfortunately, many companies have yet to discover the importance of establishing and enforcing core values. What may be worse are companies that post on the wall a list of profound words with some brief definition, then without any further action assume that everyone throughout the organization is living these "values." Harsh realities of that failed strategy appear in many ways, not the least of which are headlines appearing on the front pages of local and national newspapers.

As an example, a corporate value of excellence typically exists and is measured every month based on a spreadsheet highlighting numbers of sales. When no value of integrity exists highlighting expectations of ethical behavior, salespeople may go to extreme measure just to reach a number. Often, when decisions need to be made with values in conflict with each other, the situation can be resolved by placing the values into priority order: for instance, putting integrity at the top over excellence. When values are implemented effectively, all personnel become more professional, upholding the reputation of their company.

Legendary college basketball coach John Wooden exemplified the importance of players adhering to his values in building his extraordinary career at UCLA. He had this to say about values:

> *Leadership is more than just forcing people to do what you say…A good leader creates belief in the leader's philosophy, in the organization, in the mission. Creating belief is difficult to do where a vacuum of values exists, where the only thing that matters is the end result…whether it's beating the competition on the court or increasing the profit margins in the books.*[21]

Establishing core values that include expected behaviors for all members of your organization is one of the most important tasks for business leaders. Without core values, you accept the risk of people behaving badly, jeopardizing the organization's character, its reputation, and

---

[21] Wooden, John R., and Steve Jamison. *Wooden on Leadership*. New York: McGraw-Hill, 2005. 69.

its success. Identify your organization's values. Define the behaviors associated with each. Make it abundantly clear to all what "right" looks like when it comes to living the values. Bring the values to life through communication, sharing values-based stories, and hiring people who believe in them.

A profound example of the conflict between the values of integrity and loyalty was highlighted by a professor of ethics during an executive leadership program I attended as an army general. He shared in a presentation at this conference: "When your organization wants you to do something right, it asks for your integrity. When it wants you to do something wrong, it asks for your loyalty." This example highlights the importance of defining the behaviors associated with the value to minimize any confusion.

Live The Values

There is no better way to demonstrate values than leading by example through living them.

Behaviors are a choice. When a leader demonstrates adherence to a set of standards defined by values through his or her behavior, credibility and influence rule the day. When leaders do not do so, credibility, trust, and confidence are eroded in those who observe them.

Embodying the values in daily life means using them to make both routine and complex decisions and letting them guide your actions under normal and stressful conditions. Being open about how you use them in your decision-making will provide an example that will pay huge dividends in getting others to live them as well.

Establishing recognition programs in your business that showcase people living the values can reinforce their importance to the organization. When values come alive, a winning culture is established that helps sustain the reputation of the organization as well as retains and attracts the best people.

Within the first thirty days of my initial assignment as a fresh graduate out of West Point, I was confronted with an ethical decision regarding evaluating the readiness of my platoon of fifty soldiers. If I reported to my commander a percentage of readiness that failed to meet the established standard, that would immediately have an adverse impact on our organization in the eyes of leadership. It would also mean exposing substandard performance by my platoon and extending work hours during the week and weekend, which would have a demoralizing impact on the troops.

There was no question about the right thing to do. I reported precisely the facts on our readiness, and the extended work hours proceeded until we met the standard. For the rest of my career, I made these types of ethical decisions regularly. So did my fellow officers.

I will never forget learning the story of Lieutenant Colonel Chris Hughes, US Army, leading the 2nd Battalion, 327th Infantry during the invasion of Iraq.[22] It was April 3, 2003, when his unit entered the town square of An-Najaf, after four days of intense fighting. His primary goal was to meet with the holy man Ayatollah Ali al-Sistani, who had been held in house arrest for the past fifteen years by Saddam Hussein. Before the two had a chance to meet, Chris and his unit were met by an angry crowd who feared they were there to capture the town's holy man and destroy the Imam Ali Mosque, a holy site for Shiite Muslims around the world. Hundreds of people were protesting his arrival, instigated by agitators who were trying to make the US Military look bad in front of global media. Rocks were being thrown, twice hitting Colonel Hughes in the head. Tensions

---

[22] Hughes, Christopher P. War on Two Fronts: An infantry Commander's War in Iraq and Afghanistan, Casemate Publishers, Philadelphia, PA, 2007, p.103-114.

were rising rapidly. He had to diffuse this riot quickly or civilians were going to be hurt—possibly killed.

To the amazement of many Iraqis, Colonel Hughes directed three actions by his unit: take a knee, point weapons to the ground, and smile. Some Iraqis smiled back; some took a knee. Tensions slowly began to dissipate. Lieutenant Colonel Hughes conducted a successful withdrawal, not a single shot was fired, and no one was hurt. When his unit was safely out of harm's way, the colonel turned to face the crowd, placed his right hand over his heart and bowed—a clear act of respect for the Iraqi people. Later that evening, he learned that the Ayatollah issued a formal *fatwa*:

> *"Do not interfere with the American forces entering Iraq. Praise be to Allah, Grand Ayatollah Sistani of the Mosque of Ali."*

This event was caught on camera by the global media, catching the attention around the world, including praise by President Bush. What it highlighted was the extraordinary leadership of Colonel Hughes. In my personal conversation with him, I learned how important it was for Chris to win any fight without firing a shot, if possible. What helped him succeed in these extraordinary circumstances were his years of developmental assignments; his time in Haiti, where he learned about dealing with riots; and his ability to operationalize the army's core values of doing what was right, maintaining the moral high ground. Equally important was his comprehensive understanding of the culture and values of the Iraqi people, our future partners.

In the business or competitive sports worlds, the ethical challenges are the same. The search for effective ways to communicate, train, educate, and inspire living the values is a perpetual task. Tireless communication by leaders at all levels is key. Embedding the training and learning in professional development programs is important. Recognition and sharing stories can be very effective in demonstrating what "right" looks like. Hiring people who understand the values and expectations for their behaviors is where it all starts.

★ STORY ★

Ron Thigpen, President Of Georgia Bank And Trust, Augusta, Georgia

Ron Thigpen retired as the president of Georgia Bank and Trust, having served in that institution for twenty-five years. He was well known as an exceptional professional banker. He also enjoyed a reputation as being a humble servant-leader who cared deeply about the people in his organization and those in the community in which he lived. He had been hired as the chief operating officer of the bank three years after the bank was established.

As a relatively new bank in town, the immediate challenge was to grow the institution. In a very competitive banking environment, which consisted of other local, statewide, and national financial institutions, growth was dependent upon attracting and retaining a staff of well-qualified people who could help distinguish the bank from all others.

Knowing the real value of community banks was providing personal, responsive support to local businesses and families, Ron was tireless in acquiring people of the right quality. He led the creation, on behalf of the CEO, of the bank's core values, which included integrity, excellence, and responsiveness. He led the development of expectations for desired behaviors for each value. By modeling and living these values daily, Ron (along with the CEO and the rest of the executive leadership team) gained respect and trust throughout the organization and community. This bedrock foundation of character was fundamental to the bank's ability to create and grow one of the most successful community banks in the state of Georgia. Turnover in its leadership ranks was almost nonexistent because leaders never wanted to leave. Over the bank's twenty-eight years of existence, it grew to $1.8 billion in total assets with a staff of more than 350 people.

The values created by the leadership team were genuine. They created clarity regarding who the leaders were and defined the qualities of the people they recruited to join their team. Their slogan, "Doing the Right Thing," became one of the most recognized in the region.

College basketball coaching legend John Wooden once said: "You can't live a perfect day without doing something for someone who will never be able to repay you."[23] When I think of people who left or are leaving a wonderful legacy by the way they live, their character encapsulates the essence of that memory.

Leadership Tips—
Building Competence And Confidence

- **Discover yourself.** Be a leader of honesty and integrity. Determine what you are good at by assessing your strengths. Discover what you enjoy doing. Learn what you stand for. Learn what motivates you. Use this knowledge to help guide your everyday actions, how you interact with others, and understand where you can best contribute. Help others learn how to be most effective in communicating with you.

- **Establish and communicate core values.** Ensure your organization has clearly established core values that truly represent what is most important. Ensure behaviors are well defined for each value. Be tireless in your communication of the values until everyone gets it, and then communicate them some more.

- **Living the values.** Lead by example every day through living the values. Make decisions based on them and share the process with all. Ensure the leaders from the executive team down to first-line supervisors commit to them. Routinely recognize those who live the values.

---

[23] Wooden, John R., and Steve Jamison. *Wooden on Leadership*. New York: McGraw-Hill, 2005.

CHAPTER 4

Reveal And Reinforce Leader Competencies

Bottom Line Up Front: Reveal and reinforce leader competencies by identifying core competencies, identifying leader competencies, and making competencies visible.

Have you ever asked the question, "Where do I start learning how to become a more effective leader?" I get asked this question often in my travels around the country as I interact with businesses and professional organizations. I love it, as it is a clear sign that these folks want to grow. But it is also discouraging to hear, because the rationale for the question is most likely people getting little or no guidance from their leaders at work.

To be the best you can be, you need to know what competencies must be mastered to be successful. Leadership competencies are fundamentals, the blocking and tackling equivalents of football.

In the army, leader development begins on day one in basic training and continues throughout a career of service. To be an effective leader, you must first fully embrace and internalize what it takes to be a follower, an individual member of a team. In the business world, there is no "basic training" opportunity. The burden rests with current leaders to teach these fundamentals to future leaders.

In the army, the ability to inspire in others a commitment to grow as leaders is paramount for success. How good do you want to be? How good do you want your people to be?

Defining success as a leader should not be left up to chance. The adage "I'll know it when I see it" has never worked for the army, nor most other successful enterprises. The best people in any organization want to be successful and are genuinely interested in knowing the performance standards against which they will be measured. This chapter focuses on the need to identify leadership competencies for individual members of the team and supervisors at all levels. Reveal them. Consistently reinforce them. Bring them to life.

To assess leadership performance, there must be a standard upon which a leader's work is measured. One way to help define success from a leadership perspective is to identify competencies. Competencies are fundamentally defined by knowledge and skills. Knowledge is factual or procedural understanding of a particular subject; skills are observable behaviors gained through experience and practice.

Much has been written about the subject of competencies, behaviors, skills, attributes, etc. Do not get bogged down by the variety of interpretations or options that exist for defining them. Stay focused. Keep it simple. Make a decision about how you want to define success and get on with it.

Using well-defined competencies can help recruit the right people as well as promote the right people. Competencies also provide a clear guide on leadership goals, which should be one area of focus for individual development programs.

The army uses field manuals and other documents to define the leadership development process. These documents highlight the essential leadership competencies that define success for soldiers of all ranks. Including competencies on annual performance appraisals as clear objectives (combined with this manual, which describes the program) makes the intent to train leaders abundantly clear. The army's methodology of documenting the leadership program in a manual and a technique for assessing performance is a powerful example for any organization serious about developing leaders.

Three essential tasks will help reveal and reinforce leader competencies.

Identify Core Competencies

Clearly defined core competencies shine a bright light on what it takes to be an effective member of a team. Every person in any organization is a member of a team, whether an executive team or a small team at the lowest level.

Clearly identifying these core competencies is important, as they define success. They highlight how people will be assessed in the performance of their duties. Leaders must know them and reinforce them in their own behaviors. They also drive training and coaching priorities (discussed in later chapters). Examples include:

- Provides consistent quality work
- Works effectively with others
- Demonstrates a strong work ethic
- Is reliable
- Meets deadlines
- Follows procedures
- Demonstrates safe work practices
- Accepts responsibility
- Displays commitment to the company and team
- Seeks personal improvement
- Listens with intent to understand

Identify Leader Competencies

As you review what competencies are most important at various levels in your organization, consider who has a leading versus supporting role. For instance, there is a distinct difference in a creation versus an implementation role.

The army, as an example, defined eight core leadership competencies for all army leaders along with corresponding behaviors in the 2006 field manual.[24] The eight include: leads others, extends influence beyond the chain of command, leads by example, communicates, creates a positive environment, prepares self, develops others, and gets results.

In the best-selling book *Managing the Millennials*, the authors highlight three principal core competencies of leaders of millennials. These are adapting, communicating, and envisioning.

- **Adapting** is the willingness of the manager to accept that a millennial does not have the same experience, values, or frame of reference as members of other generations.

- **Communicating** is the ability of the manager to make a connection at a relational level, like engaging the self-absorbed or disarming the defensive.

- **Envisioning** is the manager's need to create meaning and accountability for the employee by connecting personal goals with the organization's objectives.[25]

At lower levels in the organization, a leader has daily contact with most of his or her people. These are front-line and middle-level managers who are engaged in day-to-day operations where the action is. The

---

[24] U. S. Army Field Manual 6-22: Army Leadership. Headquarters, Dept. of the Army, 2006.

[25] Espinoza, Chip, and Mick Ukleja. *Managing the Millennials: Discover the Core Competencies for Managing Today's Workforce*. John Wiley & Sons, Inc., 2016.

environment is generally less complex than at higher levels. Below are representative competencies at the middle levels:

- Provides direct guidance
- Achieves results
- Inspires and motivates
- Exercises compassion
- Sets clear goals
- Develops others
- Communicates effectively
- Listens with intent to understand
- Enforces discipline and adherence to standards
- Shows gratitude
- Manages conflict
- Treats people with respect
- Makes good decisions
- Holds people accountable
- Delegates effectively
- Implements policies and procedures
- Maintains a positive role model
- Builds cohesion

Enforcing accountability was a critical leadership task that was not easy for me initially, but necessary to master if I was going to be successful in the army. My first real test began the day I arrived as a brand-new lieutenant to first duty assignment at Fort Bragg, North Carolina. I was given the task of determining if my platoon sergeant, second-in-command of my platoon of fifty soldiers, was worthy of keeping his position and suitable for future service in the army. Staff Sergeant Jones (not his real name) was my platoon sergeant. He had been in the army for fourteen years, served three combat tours in Vietnam, and was one of the most decorated soldiers in the entire brigade of 2,500 troops. He was a technical genius, able to install, operate, and maintain all of our equipment like no other.

However, he was a terrible leader of the troops. The platoon was in a state of chaos and unable to perform its mission. Sergeant Jones was abusive to the troops. He was unreliable, untrustworthy, and had no idea how to train others. No one in the organization trusted or respected him. He also had a host of personal challenges, including massive indebtedness and dependency on alcohol. In retrospect, he most likely suffered from post-traumatic stress disorder, but we did not know it at the time. All eyes were on me; everyone knew the situation.

I was fortunate to have had a great boss in Captain Thom Tuckey who became one of my most trusted advisors throughout my military career. He and other leaders helped coach me through the Jones challenge. I spent considerable time with Sergeant Jones, attempting to orchestrate changes in his leadership behaviors and helping get his personal life in order. He successfully completed a three-week inpatient alcohol abuse program. He made some progress, but ultimately was unable to overcome his own demons. As a result of his failure to perform to the standard necessary to lead soldiers, I had to recommend he be relieved of his duties. He was reassigned out of the unit to a position where he had no supervisory responsibilities but could contribute his technical skills until his contract with the army was fulfilled.

As one progresses upward in the organization, a leader's responsibilities change, and so do competencies. There often is overlap in these lists.

At the senior or executive level, the environment is characterized by increased complexity, higher risk, greater uncertainty, and less direct control over subordinate echelons. According to research by Navalent, between 50–70 percent of executives fail within the first eighteen months of promotion into an executive role, either coming from within or from outside the organization. Getting these competencies right can make or break an organization.[26]

Representative competencies at these higher levels include:

- Treats people with respect
- Delegates effectively
- Holds people accountable
- Sets vision and mission
- Provides strategic direction
- Communicates intent
- Clarifies roles and responsibilities
- Shapes the organizational climate and culture
- Makes good decisions
- Allocates resources
- Leads change
- Exercises humility
- Synchronizes actions
- Designs organizations and structures
- Develops policies and procedures
- Builds partnerships
- Possesses executive presence

Some of these tasks cannot be delegated; some can. Some can be found at multiple levels in the organization. Clarification of responsibility can be a significant contributor to the success of an organization.

---

[26] Carucci, Ron A., and Eric C. Hansen. "Rising to Power: The Journey of Exceptional Executives." Navalent, 2014. http://www.navalent.com.

One of the most challenging leadership skills impacting executives is the ability to listen. As we reach these high levels of authority, we struggle with holding back on telling people how smart we are. Many new executives tend to rely on how they achieved success in the past, struggling with adapting to new conditions and environments. I learned a wonderful analogy about listening from another important mentor in my life, Major General Perry Smith (USAF, retired). He calls effective listening "squinting with your ears." Squinting with our ears will help build trust with your people essential for achieving long-term success.

Make Competencies Visible

Inspire growth by bringing leadership competencies to life; make them visible and the subject of conversations between team leaders and team members on a regular and consistent basis. Competencies are much like values, and attention to both can help you set the conditions for achieving extraordinary success.

Start by making competencies visible by documenting them in your employee handbook. Make sure all employees are well-versed in the contents of this manual through initial orientations and regular performance reviews.

Continue making them visible by explicitly including leadership competencies in your annual performance appraisals. When competencies are visible in manuals and included in performance evaluations, CEOs and business leaders make clear their intent to help people understand how success is defined. This clarity also helps set the conditions for placing people into positions where they can be most effective for the company.

Documenting competencies is fundamental to success, but insufficient by itself. The final element of visibility comes when leaders engage their people in assessments of competencies through coaching sessions throughout the year. Frequent feedback, ongoing check-ins, and regularly scheduled coaching sessions reinforce the importance of leadership competencies. More details on coaching can be found in chapter 6.

What are the consequences of promoting people who do not have the leadership skills to be effective in the new position (or the aptitude to learn them)? I would suggest most of you have experienced such a situation, unfortunately. As organizations grow in size and complexity, identifying high-potential performers takes on an increased level of importance. Having a documented history of sustained excellent performance can be of enormous value in making good personnel decisions. By the same token, documenting poor performance helps identify those employees who need to be let go.

⋆ STORY ⋆

Jeff Bevis, Founder And CEO Of FirstLight Home Care, Cincinnati, Ohio

Jeff Bevis is the inspirational leader and CEO of FirstLight Home Care. This company is a franchise system providing nonmedical in-home care for seniors, the disabled, retired and injured veterans, and others needing assistance. The demand for these services continues to rise across the country. Bevis is tireless in his quest to understand and meet the needs of these people.

Providing consistent, quality home care is not easy. As a seasoned veteran of the franchise world, Bevis recognized his monumental task: finding the right candidates to become members of his executive team and FirstLight owners.

Bevis knew for the organization to provide consistent, quality care, he needed to define the leader competencies essential for owner and leadership staff success. At the very core of his vision was the need to embrace servant leadership. To provide high-quality, personalized care for each client family member, every franchisee (or owner) must lead with common purpose, possess great listening skills, exercise respect and compassion, and ultimately deliver exceptional care.

There were significant challenges at both the corporate and owner levels. Bevis first had to develop his executive leadership team and focus on their leadership competencies, which included the creation and communication of a vision for FirstLight, along with the establishment of a comprehensive culture of care. He then developed and distributed the set of standards for business tools, processes, and systems to enable an owner to be successful.

At the ownership level, often new owners would struggle in the early months of operation. This struggle led to declining confidence, questioning their own abilities, or wondering whether they could effectively find strong demand for services. In these pivotal times, Bevis and his executive leaders demonstrated the same fundamental leadership competencies that owners had to master with clients' families. These competencies included listening skills, patience, and respect for each owner's scenario and unique challenges. By exercising these competencies, confidence within the owners increased, owners' faith in their own abilities was restored, and the owners' focus to stay the course to achieve business success was renewed.

Well-defined leadership competencies became one of the critical elements enabling Jeff Bevis to achieve success in building FirstLight's culture of care. It took years for Bevis to grow the organization to its current level: 170 independent franchise owners and still growing.

Many leadership competencies merit consideration for you and your organization. Prioritize. Choose the ones that are most important.

There will inevitably be some frustration in trying to determine the perfect list. In the army, we use the phrase "move out and draw fire" when we make decisions knowing they are imperfect. Make the best decision you can with the information and time available. Over time, you can refine and improve the list.

Identification of leadership competencies is the easy part. Gaining proficiency in them requires discipline, systematic training, tireless practice, and honest feedback.

Once the competencies are well documented, the need for a plan to develop them in your people becomes the priority. That plan is the subject of the next chapter.

Leadership Tips—
Building Competence And Confidence

- **Identify core competencies.** Clearly identify the key competencies that every individual member of the team needs to learn.

- **Identify leader's competencies.** Clearly identify the most important leadership competencies managers at all levels must learn, including the executive level leaders.

- **Make competencies visible.** Inspire growth by bringing these competencies to life. Clearly document them in employee handbooks. Integrate them into the performance appraisal system. Highlight them during regular scheduled coaching sessions and group meetings.

CHAPTER 5

Attack With A Leader Development Program

Bottom Line Up Front: Attack with a leader development program by determining the goals of your leader development program, determining how you will accomplish the goals, then executing and sustaining the program.

I n the words of General Creighton Abrams, former US Army chief of staff: "Soldiers are not *in* the army. Soldiers *are* the army."[27]

The leader development program in the army is comprehensive, holistic, and lifelong. The army recognizes that leaders do not drift to greatness; they achieve it through tireless pursuit of learning and growing. Effective delegation to the lowest levels is paramount for the army to be the adaptive, agile force needed to accomplish its mission.

The army does not hire leaders from the outside to lead its deployable formations. The army also does not have professional privates or lieutenants. Soldiers either get promoted or leave—it is either *up* or *out*. That is why the US Army invests millions of dollars in the professional development of leaders at all ranks, from sergeant to general. And yes,

---

[27] Sorely, Lewis. A Better War: the Unexamined Victories and Final Tragedy of America's Last Years in Vietnam. Orlando: Harvest Book, 1999, P. 360..

many of those leaders depart the service before retirement, as only the most qualified get promoted. Some may ask if the investment is wasted on those who depart. The answer is no, because the army cannot afford to have leaders in the ranks who are not trained, educated, and developed. It is that simple. There is also the altruistic reason: the army's desire to return soldiers to civilian life better able to make a positive impact in their communities.

Many business leaders do not hesitate to invest in technical competency training for their people to ensure job proficiency. Those leaders who are serious about setting the conditions for long term success invest in the leader development of their people. Programs that include educating, developing, and coaching can become the catalyst that ignites an organization into truly becoming a great place to work. Business leaders cannot ignore this task and expect to achieve sustained levels of high performance from their people. Without any development program, a culture of mediocrity will prevail.

In 2012, The Procter and Gamble Company, with Bob McDonald as its chairman, president, and CEO, ranked number one in *Chief Executive*'s list of "The 40 Best Companies for Leaders."[28] McDonald was praised for the organization's creation of the general manager college and continued involvement in their hands-on training. One of the most significant initiatives was a values-based leadership curriculum in which Bob personally trained more than 250 of his senior leaders. P&G has long been an investor in developing leaders. Under Bob's leadership, the strategy was expanded to become the *5E Model*, which focused on training everyone on the behaviors of leadership: *E*nvision, *E*ngage, *E*nergize, *E*nable, and *E*xecute. A wide range of development resources for this model and other key aspects of the strategy are available and used to help employees at all levels at P&G.

---

[28] "Procter & Gamble Voted Top Company For Leadership Development | Newsroom." Russell Reynolds Associates. 2012. Accessed December 17, 2018. https://www.russellreynolds.com/newsroom/procter-gamble-voted-top-company-for-leadership-development.

Investing in developing people sends a clear message that leaders care. Employee respect for and confidence in leadership grows when there is a well-thought-out program focused on their development. When programs are put in writing, people take them seriously; they become real.

I first learned of the concept of using the appropriate leadership style based on situations while attending a ten-month army school for majors in 1989. The course was titled "Fundamentals of Senior-Level Leadership in Peace and War (P913)."[29] The actual lesson was called "A Situational Approach to Leader Development," by Major Keith L. Kettler and Dr. Ken Blanchard. This model was initially developed by both Blanchard and Dr. Paul Hersey in the late 1960s.[30] The fundamental concept I learned from this lesson was this: There is no single best style of leadership. Rather, the best leaders adopt the most appropriate style to meet the needs of their followers based on their diagnosis of the individual's ability and willingness to conquer a task.

In all honesty, I wish I had paid more attention to that methodology, as it would have made me a much more effective leader much earlier in my career.

Based on the resources available and priorities of the company, craft a program that puts it all together. Focus on twelve months at a time. Be innovative in your approach. Don't get bogged down in the creation of the perfect program that could win a literary prize for prose but take forever in publishing. Keep it straightforward, adaptable, achievable, and sustainable. Make a decision and get after it. Adjust in the future based on feedback from your people being trained.

---

[29] Fundamentals of Senior-level Leadership in Peace and War: P913: Advance Sheet Booklet. Fort Leavenworth, Kansas: U.S. Army Command and General Staff College, 1989.

[30] Hersey, Paul, Ken Blanchard, and Dewey E. Johnson. Management of Organizational Behavior, 10th Edition. New York: Pearson, 2013.

There is a high risk for any business leader in assuming that people inherently know how to lead others. What follows are three key tasks that can help you develop and execute a successful program.

Determine The Goals Of Your Leader Development Program

There is a great saying: If you don't know where you are going, any path will get you there. The most important first step in creating a leader development program is to clarify the goals of the program. Analyze your vision of where you want your company to be in the next three to five years, your mission (why you exist), and your specific company objectives for the next twelve to twenty-four months. Your leadership goals need to be directly tied to these three.

Identify executive leadership goals. The senior leaders of any organization, new or seasoned, need continuous development, in many cases even more than others. As an example, from my army experience, even after I was promoted to general, I attended many executive leadership programs. The agendas were carefully crafted to accomplish different objectives, all designed to help me be successful as an executive in the army. The skills needed to be successful at the executive level may differ from the skills the new leaders master to reach that level.

- Identify goals derived from assessment of performance. Insights are gained through observation, coaching, and evaluation of performance. Results generate goals for professional development opportunities at all levels.

- Identify goals for supervisors. This includes executive level down to first line supervisors. Newly promoted supervisors merit special attention. When members of the team are promoted to supervisor, the organization needs to help enable their success. Doing nothing sets up a newly promoted person for failure.

- Identify goals for high-potential performers. Creating a pipeline for future leaders of the company is a critical task. This includes the need to identify who the high-potential performers are, and what is needed to set them up for success in the future.

- Identify goals for unique or special positions. There will likely be unique leadership goals for positions like HR, sales, marketing, logistics, research, or others. Goals for new general managers or positions where a significant change in roles of the organization or significant increases in responsibility should be identified.

As an example, when I was selected by the army to command (like a CEO) an army battalion as a lieutenant colonel, additional "pre-command" training and education took place. This preparation lasted six weeks, all of it executed *before* I ever transitioned into the command position. The goal was to set the conditions for my success from day one on the new job. Today, the army trains approximately 2,000 senior leaders in this program *every year*. The vast majority of these leaders are going to be "CEOs" of army organizations ranging in size from 750 to 3,000 people. This preparation is *in addition to* the many years of experience in developmental jobs designed to build competency and confidence. The lesson to be learned here is to look carefully at key positions in your organization to determine what can and should be done to help prepare them for success.

Determine How You Will Accomplish The Goals

Once goals are established, the next task is to determine the methods and techniques to address them. There is a need to put this program in writing to address all the goals, in priority, and secure absolute endorsement by senior leaders.

The US Army invests in three distinct approaches to developing leaders: Institutional programs are mandated by the army leadership, are applied across the entire force, and are generally focused on formal education and training based on rank, promotions, and assignments. Organizational-level leader development is the second approach and includes on-the-job training, coaching, experiential assignments, and other initiatives implemented by local commanders tailored to the needs of the unit. The third approach is self-leadership, whereby the army expects every leader to invest in independent learning through reading, virtual training and education programs, or other individual initiatives.

For business leaders, one approach does not work for everyone. Each organization must customize its approach to developing leaders based on the priorities and needs of the organization and the available resources.

To design an effective program, consider breaking down the big task into smaller elements, similar to how the army uses its three-pronged approach. If you are part of a large corporation, there will likely be investments at the corporate level to address some of the goals. If your organization is smaller, then the entire program will be the responsibility of the CEO or president or business owner.

Formal programs will include outsourced training programs, professional organization memberships, conferences, contracted or formal internal workshops, well-defined and mandated internal programs, and even executive coaching. There are many world class training companies that have proven curriculums that can help leaders become more effective at leading and coaching their people. These opportunities need to be considered in your assessment. You should also consider bringing the training to your company location, where more folks can reap the benefits of the investment. Many professional training organizations offer train-the-trainer programs, which could provide significant return-on-investment through developing expertise that resides within your company.

Informal programs will include on-the-job training, experiential learning, stretch assignments, special projects, coaching, and mentoring. Taking advantage of expertise and special talent within the company is a great way help develop leaders. When spearheaded by qualified facilitators, these experiences can be rewarding for the trainees as well as the trainer. Identifying leaders within the company to orchestrate sustainment programs that compliment or reinforce formal training events can be a huge benefit to all. Create opportunities for leaders to share best practices through vignettes or case studies, or even to discuss books.

Self-initiated programs will include attending college, reading good books, and taking initiative on changing behaviors based on 360° or other types of assessments. Much can be learned by reading, as authors of books can become "virtual coaches," sharing best practices along with tools and techniques that worked for them. I have included some of my favorite leadership books in Appendix G.

Within the organization, leadership programs can be created and led by competent members of the company. There are likely people in your organization who are (or desire to become) experts and thrive in these types of assignments. Discover who they are and deputize them.

Coaching one-on-one remains one of the most effective methods to help develop leaders, when it is performed by those who are proficient in the task. Coaching, in this situation, is defined by those leaders who have direct reports with the obligation to develop their people. No coaching or bad coaching is a problem. Effective coaching is so critical that I have devoted an entire chapter to it (chapter 6).

To help reduce the fiscal cost of training events, consider collaborating with other companies in your geographic region that may have the same needs and would be willing to partner with you to share expenses and experiences.

The idea of technology as a mere tool is long gone; it is an *environment* and is expected to be integrated into any development program. Many professional leadership training companies integrate virtual training into their offerings. Take advantage of it.

Decision-making is among the most critical skills effective leaders at all levels must learn. Mastery is gained through use of a proven process and experience. Decades ago, the army established a standard methodology called "military decision-making process" or MDMP.[31] MDMP is the army's approach to problem-solving. It is a methodology that evolved over decades of use, a valuable tool to help commanders and staff at all levels assess situations and develop comprehensive, achievable courses of action designed to accomplish a specific mission. Military operations are inherently complex, even at the lowest levels. Great emphasis is placed on leaders' responsibility and a process to make good decisions, especially when time is of the essence. I was introduced to MDMP as a brand-new lieutenant out of West Point and used it throughout my entire thirty-two-year career of military service.

Balancing intuition and analysis are critical to making good decisions. Give people, especially those high-potential performers, the experience of participating or leading the decision-making process. Experience is how people gain competence and confidence in their analysis and gut feel for decisions. (A more in-depth description of the MDMP, with a translation for business application, can be found in Appendix F.)

---

[31] U.S. Army Field Manual 101-5, Staff Organization and Operations. Washington, DC: Headquarters, Dept. of the Army, 1997.

When appropriate and feasible, consider rotation programs that place current or up-and-coming leaders into positions throughout your company to help them experience other aspects of the profession.

Mentoring programs can also be highly effective in helping to guide leadership growth. One significant advantage is that most mentors are not in the chain of command, which affords a more open, honest environment for dialogue. Mentors are volunteers, as are mentees. When leaders are willing to assume the responsibility and interested members of the organization seek mentorship, great partnerships can emerge.

Execute And Sustain The Program

Execute the program, period. Wonderfully crafted programs that sit idle on a shelf or in some hidden file provide no benefit. There *will* be inevitable distractions, budget cuts, and competing demands that threaten to derail portions of the program. Make leader development a priority. Consider competing demands when drafting your program so that it can proceed at some level even during the toughest times. You do not want your people to believe that you are not serious about training leaders.

One profound reason the army enjoys long-term success in developing great leaders is its fundamental commitment of resources to the task. Leader development is a priority. Programs continue year after year, even during times of war. Business leaders must take this same approach.

Sustainment is inherent in every successful development strategy. Constant practice and experiential learning cement the concepts learned through actual focused training or educational programs. Deliberate activities and methods ensure that people apply what they have learned. Reinforcement strategies include refresher initiatives, sustainability modules, action plan implementation, connecting new behaviors to performance appraisal systems, and adopting best practices. Coaching is at the foundation of all sustainment. Training is not a one-time event—rather, it is an ongoing process that enables refinement of skills and behaviors over time.

Senior leaders must buy into and support the program, securing the resources necessary for success. Think beyond today—look deep. Set aside resources in the future to help achieve the goals in this program.

Failure to address sustainment will result in lost leadership capacity and the erosion of skills learned during the initial training program. Sustainment is the basis of maximizing return-on-investment of the leadership development strategy.

Review the health of the organization's leader development program at least annually. Ensure it remains in sync with the company's needs, is having a positive impact on performance, and is ultimately increasing the results of the company.

⋆ STORY ⋆

Jeff Rowe, CEO of Hydro Systems, Cincinnati, Ohio

Jeff Rowe was a successful CEO of Hydro Systems, a $50 million manufacturing company headquartered in the United States. He was a passionate leader, a gifted communicator, and genuinely cared about his organization of 200 people. His company developed cutting-edge technology that focused on safer operations in chemical injecting and dispensing systems for a variety of industries including horticulture, dairy, food service, animal health, and water treatment.

But Jeff Rowe had a problem. The challenge came when the global demand for the company's products grew rapidly, exceeding its capacity to deliver by a large margin. Rowe had to make a decision about how he was going to grow rapidly to help protect his people in their daily handling of hazardous chemicals. Rowe recognized the key to growing his organization while maintaining the quality of products and services was his people.

He tasked his leadership experts, Fran Nunan and Gail Love, to develop a comprehensive leadership development program to increase the competence and confidence of his people. He did not make the common mistake of just hiring and promoting more people into leadership positions without preparing them for success.

The development program initially focused on shop supervisors who were being promoted into increasingly responsible roles. It was later expanded to leaders at all levels throughout the organization. Rowe describes the impact of this initiative:

"Everyone in a management role at Hydro suddenly wanted to get in to one of our leadership development classes. Getting accepted to a class became a badge of honor, as our folks saw those being taught the leadership lessons getting promoted and taking on challenging rotational assignments. The program became a recruiting advantage, bringing in more highly skilled talent with more ambition who crave development and advancement. These great people helped us to grow our business at a rate much faster than we could have previously imagined."[32]

The results of this deliberate investment in developing his people had a profound impact on the company. The company doubled in size and achieved its growth goals of $100M in eight years. The top- and bottom-line results improved EBITDA by multiples. The company also built a deep bench of talent, and turnover among the top talent group virtually disappeared.

Leadership Tips—
Building Competence And Confidence

- **Determine the goals of your leader development program.** Use the company's vision, mission, and business objectives as the foundation for establishing goals. Perform comprehensive assessments on the individuals' leader competencies that highlight gaps in skills needed to accomplish the mission. Based on your assessments, derive goals for the program, document them in writing, and share them with all.

- **Determine how you will accomplish the goals**. Determine the best combination of training and education, experiential learning and coaching to achieve the goals. Use standard development tools to help create repeatable processes to maximize learning. Consider tailored programs for high-potential performers and those selected for promotion into critical leadership positions.

- **Execute and sustain the program.** Execute the program. Reassess periodically to ensure the program is meeting its goals and enhancing performance of leaders and the organization. Sustain your program by committing resources in the future to achieve a culture of learning.

CHAPTER 6

Value Coaching Excellence

__Bottom Line Up Front__: Value coaching excellence by establishing a standard approach to coaching sessions, establishing goals and strategies to achieve, and enforcing accountability by assessing performance.

The year was 2003. I remember sitting nervously in the large conference room at Fort Leavenworth in Kansas, the premier army leader development installation. I was attending my first (of many) executive leadership program upon being promoted to general. I was humbled by the honor of the promotion and anxious to learn what I needed to know to be successful as a general. I had the great pleasure of meeting Dr. Marshall Goldsmith at that event, one of the top executive coaches in America. He volunteered his time to coach us on how to transition to being an effective general officer.

I still have pages of notes from the many sessions with Marshall. The fundamental takeaway from his presentations was that the leadership skills that enabled us to achieve the rank of general may not be all the skills we needed to master to be successful at this new level. What I learned from Marshall guided me from that day forward, and still do today. My trust and admiration for Marshall was one of the main reasons I pursued his Stakeholder Centered Coaching methodology as the foundation for my leadership coaching practice today.

I define coaching as the actions of a person in a leadership role who enhances the performance and development of others through teaching, training, directing, encouraging, or collaborating. Every supervisor or manager has a coaching responsibility.

During one of the most challenging times of my life, I was fortunate to have a competent, caring, committed coach in Lieutenant Colonel Bob Fasulo. It was the summer of 1990; Saddam Hussein had just invaded Kuwait. About the same time, I reported for duty as an army major in my new unit in Stuttgart, Germany. Shortly after my arrival, I learned we were going to war. Over the next six weeks, I discovered the enormous list of technical skills I would need to learn before deploying.

My supervisor, Colonel Fasulo, took me under his wing. He invested time to get to know me both personally and professionally. He gave me clear guidance on my roles and responsibilities, along with clear objectives to get me ready for deployment. He secured additional personnel he knew I would need for my staff to be successful. He ensured I received focused training in specific technical areas as required. He invested significant personal time on nights and weekends to help me learn about my people, their skills, and their strengths. He allowed me to learn from my mistakes. I learned to trust him; he learned to trust me. The coaching lessons I learned from him throughout the war stayed with me for the rest of my career and remain with me still today.

I will never forget Colonel Fasulo. I will never forget my coaches in football, basketball, and baseball. I will never forget my supervisors in my professional career, both the good ones and otherwise. Your people will never forget you either. The question is, how will they remember you?

Effective one-on-one coaching is one of the most important skills a great leader must possess. It takes discipline and practice. High performing teams are achieved with great coaches. It is difficult to become an effective coach if you have never had an effective coach.

When there is no effective coaching, the drive for high performance diminishes. A culture of mediocrity evolves as building competence is left up to chance. Trust slowly evaporates because people don't think their leaders care. Without direction, the inspiration to act ethically to achieve goals tapers. Excuses regarding why people can't achieve results become the norm, versus finding ways to make things happen. Who is responsible for what becomes blurry. The focus on the future is lost because leaders are too busy chasing crises.

Ineffective coaching or a lack of it will turn away new recruits and cause the best, most motivated people to leave the organization.

Effective coaching begins inside your heart. You must believe that you can have an impact in this world, that you can inspire others to achieve goals they might not otherwise attain on their own. You must commit yourself to learning how to be the best coach you can be. This positive attitude must exude from your daily actions. The real question is not *if* you will make a difference, but *what* difference you will make.

You must be committed to investing quality time with your people. This commitment was one of the toughest challenges for me, as my to-do list would take every available minute of my day if I was not careful. The competition for my time was intense. Every leadership position I occupied demanded more important work than time allowed. Constant prioritization was the order of the day. When the ultimate challenge of going to war surfaced, the tasks grew exponentially. Achieving balance is crucial. It is during the most stressful times that your people need you the most. Find ways to make yourself available for your people.

A final preparation for setting the conditions for a successful coaching experience is creating an open communications environment where honest dialogue can take place between you and your people.

The 2016 Deloitte study revealed this about millennials: "In the millennial's ideal work week, there would be significantly more time devoted to the discussion on new ideas and ways of working, on coaching and mentoring, and on the development of their leadership skills."[33]

The army grows its own leaders for tomorrow, at every rank from sergeant to general. Army culture relies on every leader coaching subordinates to be successful by earning promotions. The army's succession strategy is truly based on the foundation of leaders developing their people.

Business leaders must be able to determine if becoming a manager is in an individual's desired career path and if she has the capability to perform well in that role. Not all physicians want to be chiefs of clinics; not all salespeople want to be sales managers; not all technicians want to be shop foremen. Costs, both monetary and in trust, can be exorbitant to an organization that wrongly promotes someone into a management position.

When you establish an open communications environment, you help people get to know you, how you think, and what values inside your heart guide how you act. People listen to and follow leaders they trust. They engage in meaningful dialogue with people they trust. They are not afraid to respectfully disagree with people they trust.

Lieutenant Colonel Bryan Ellis was deputy commander (second in command of my brigade of 2,500 soldiers) when I was a colonel and the commanding officer (CEO). I had many great advisors, but Lieutenant Colonel Ellis stood out as one of my most trusted. He had a marvelous

---

[33] Deloitte Touche Tohmatsu Limited. "The 2016 Deloitte Millennial Survey: Winning Over the Next Generation of Leaders." Deloitte.com. Accessed February 22, 2019 https://www2.deloitte.com/content/dam/Deloitte/global/Documents/About-Deloitte/gx-millenial-survey-2016-exec-summary.pdf.

ability to effectively communicate with me, sharing on many occasions his honest, candid advice on decisions I needed to make. He made sure I understood the truth of what was going on in the organization. He was graceful and diplomatic when he disagreed with my ideas. I sought his advice and counsel often. He helped prevent me from making bad decisions. He was a monumental contributor to my success.

On the flip side, the lack of open communication leads to critical information never being shared. When leaders yell or criticize their employees in open forums, dominate meetings with lengthy dialog letting people know how smart they are, or shoot the messengers of bad news, then effective communication comes to a halt. The leader has created an environment where trust erodes and inspiration among members of the team to do their best disappears. The impact of bad news gets worse.

Style, grace, poise, sense of humor, and a smile go a long way toward creating the atmosphere that enhances communication. I had bosses who never got up from behind their desks to meet with me, never asked any questions, and never could stop focusing on themselves. I had other senior officers seek me out to solicit my feedback on an issue or challenge because they valued my opinion.

Meeting with your people regularly helps to break down barriers. Meet in the office, on the manufacturing floor, outside the operating room, in the cafeteria, or at the warehouse. Take advantage of opportunities to communicate outside the work area, like at the fitness center, grocery store, or the kids' soccer game. Seek out ways to learn about your people. In the army, soldiers live life together through field exercises and deployments. Find ways to live life together in business as well.

Attitude is the foundation for how one thinks about and approaches life. A positive attitude is contagious; it can change everything you do and everyone you meet. A positive attitude can bring hope to challenging situations. A positive attitude takes courage, especially when obstacles are thrown in the path. In the army, every deployment to the field presented a host of issues and unknowns, from what the enemy was going to do to the impacts of weather. Diligent training and practice help military leaders gain confidence in their ability to lead their units to mission accomplishment under any circumstances.

The business world also enjoys issues and unknowns in daily operations. People in the business world need leaders who are confident in their ability to lead, who are able to adapt to changing conditions, not just in ordinary times, but in extraordinary times. Give your leaders repeated opportunities to prove themselves by leading teams in a specific task or working alongside a senior leader in a major decision effort.

One thing stands out in my mind over my entire military career: I had people who believed in me and did not hesitate to show it. I had leaders who were more confident in my abilities than I was. They saw things in me that I did not see, that I could not visualize, that I could not appreciate. This optimism helped me become more competent and confident in my abilities as an army officer.

I learned to value the idea that successful people discover what *they* are good at, while successful leaders discover what *others* are good at.

I benefitted greatly from so many coaches who invested time in me. Unfortunately, I also had coaches who never took an active interest. It became clear to me that I was most inspired by leaders who took time to engage me after my arrival in the organization and regularly thereafter. These valuable engagements provided the example of what "right" looks like and what I tried to emulate in my role as a coach.

So, what does it take to be a successful coach? The best coaches I have known rigorously practice three main skills.

Establish A Standard Approach To Coaching Sessions

Create a standard approach to how you conduct your periodic coaching sessions, tailored to meet the needs of your people. Be clear on your agenda regarding what needs to be discussed and how you plan to execute. Be consistent in your execution. Practice the same approach so you get comfortable with it. Prepare. Find ways to seek the truth. Focus on achieving results.

Your approach to coaching different groups of people will be fundamentally the same in that you want to cause them to think. The vastly different experience levels of your people, however, will require some tailoring of your approach to best meet the individuals' needs. As an example, my coaching of brand-new lieutenants was different in many ways than my coaching of seasoned officers who had been in the army for ten or more years. My approach in coaching senior leaders when I was a general was different as well, as we focused on different competencies and different priorities.

Effective communication has both *transmit* and *receive* elements; the key is to *connect*. Behavioral preference assessments are popular in the business world today for good reason. When used correctly, these assessments become effective tools that help people connect through understanding their own behavioral tendencies and those of others. For instance, from an *Everything DiSC* assessment, one of your direct reports is a strong D style. Generally speaking, having a D style means she likes to get right to the point, is results-oriented, and is not a big fan of long, spirited discussions.[34] This is a simple example but knowing these insights about those you lead and those you work for can help you be more effective in your communication with them.

---

[34] "About Everything DiSC: Theory and History." John Wiley and Sons, Inc. Accessed February 22, 2019. https://www.everythingdisc.com/EverythingDiSC/media/SiteFiles/Assets/History/Everything-DiSC-resources-aboutdisc.pdf.

More formal, regularly scheduled one-on-one check-ins or meetings are also critical to long-term development. Scheduling these sessions adds predictability and discipline. When a rhythm is established, people begin to anticipate and better prepare for the sessions. Coaching sessions in an office setting offer the environment where a comprehensive review of goals and strategies can take place. Some goals may be best assessed through a periodic monthly or quarterly feedback process. Others, like leadership behavior changes, will likely need a more rigorous, consistent feedback process to achieve real change.

At the beginning of each year or reporting period, it pays huge dividends to have that initial coaching session where goals and strategies are reviewed, well understood, and agreed upon. A good general sequence of tasks to include in your periodic coaching sessions is outlined below:

- First, establish (if the first session of the reporting period) or review the individual's goals, ensuring they are/remain aligned with the vision, mission, and priority objectives of the organization.

- Second, discuss what is going well. Seek the individual's response to what is going well before you offer your assessment. Acknowledge and celebrate successes. Often, I have simply asked for three items here.

- Third, discuss the challenges or areas for improvement. Seek the individual's response to what is not going well before you offer your assessment. Where do both the coach and the individual agree on challenges? What are the disagreements? Underwrite honest mistakes in the pursuit of excellence so people can learn. Learn the rationale for any shortfall in the individual's ability or desire to achieve the goal. Collaborate to develop a focused action plan that addresses how to overcome shortfalls.

- Fourth, seek suggestions for how you, the coach, can be a more effective leader for the person being coached. Doing so will enhance trust in you and help build confidence in the individual's own capabilities.

Egos get in the way for many leaders, especially as they grow in rank or stature. When egos are alive and well, listening ceases and the effective coaching environment disappears. People suffer. Organizations suffer. At times, I have contributed to these types of negative environments. I certainly have experienced this kind of poor environment in the military created by others. I have also experienced very positive environments created by leaders who had their egos in check, who listened, and who welcomed disagreement. I was not always a good coach (I am still working on it). I had to learn how not to show people how smart I was.

Establish Agreed-Upon Goals And Strategies To Achieve

During the initial coaching session of the year with your people, you address the foundation for the year's goals or objectives, along with strategies. This initial meeting is critical to set expectations surrounding performance and to reinforce what success looks like. Most people want to be clear about their goals as an individual and, if appropriate, the leader of a team. People are more inspired to pursue their goals if they have a voice in their creation. Assigning authority along with responsibility for specific goals helps ensure individuals can create success themselves.

The leading words *create*, *build*, *develop*, *design*, and *produce* are each effective in describing specific goals for an individual with additional details: what, and by when. Examples of goals include the production of deliverables like reports or standard operating procedures, tasks, or projects to complete. Other valuable goals may focus on learning a new process or increasing proficiency on leadership competencies (see chapter 4), all of which directly impact growing as a leader.

Consider this example from the health care industry, in which a seasoned surgeon is coaching a new, inexperienced surgeon on how to perform a new procedure. The new physician is not yet competent to perform the task but is genuinely interested in learning how. In this situation, the coach will teach the new procedure by providing very focused, directive instructions to the new surgeon. As the new surgeon gains proficiency in that task, the coach transitions to more supportive behaviors like observing, correcting when necessary, and reinforcing good work. Over- or undersupervising people can be huge demoralizers.

When I received clear guidance on goals from my supervisor, a sense of relief came to me as the fog cleared. Most goals from my army experience were put in writing on a development plan for me for the upcoming year. I learned what was expected of me. I enjoyed this experience as a brand-new lieutenant fresh out of college as well as a colonel with over twenty-two years on active duty. And I was also grateful that my supervisors cared enough to make it clear for me. While I was far from perfect, I did my best to carry these best practices throughout my career. When I did, my people were always grateful.

At other times, my bosses did nothing in the way of establishing goals for me or spending time coaching me. Needless to say, these were not my favorite bosses.

I was also grateful to my supervisors when we discussed strategies to achieve goals. In many cases, I did not need additional guidance, but in others I needed a lot. It was important for me to know where to seek additional help if I needed it.

One of the most important responsibilities of a coach is to discover the career aspirations of direct reports. To initiate that conversation, I often asked, "Where do you want to be five years from now?" I learned this approach when I was a young army captain serving in South Korea. A senior officer invited me into his office, pulled out a legal pad of paper, turned it 90 degrees, and penciled in a five-year road map for me. He highlighted the decision points I would face and options available down each path. I have used that same technique for decades to help others gain clarity, just as I did, on options for the future.

Enforce Accountability By Assessing Performance

In the army, there is no room for soldiers who cannot be relied upon to perform their duties to standard. Army organizations can only be successful if each and every soldier does his or her individual job. In the business environment, the same is true.

Accountability is best achieved when every leader in the organization feels comfortable holding each other accountable. Accountability starts at the highest levels. If the senior leader does not hold his executive team accountable, subordinate leaders are likely to think, "If the boss does not care, why should I?"

According to the 2016 Deloitte study on millennials referenced earlier, young workers actually want to stay with organizations in greater numbers when they are held accountable for their performance.

Effective coaching demands the objective assessment of performance. Without this assessment, no system of accountability will be achieved. Assessments help people learn what they are doing well and what needs to improve. They also help leaders learn priorities for training and development. Leaders genuinely interested in growing cannot be shy about seeking honest feedback on their performance and then taking action to address deficiencies.

The army has quite effectively used a formal performance appraisal system for soldiers of all ranks for decades. The appraisal is a two-page report and has endured small changes over time. The actual report is accompanied by what is called a "support form" which contains key roles and responsibilities as well as specific goals for the upcoming reporting period, usually a year. The support form is a tool designed to help managers conduct periodic coaching sessions with their people, tracking progress or areas for improvement. Oftentimes, I shared *my* own support form agreed upon with my supervisor, with my own direct reports to ensure they had clarity on my goals for the year. This knowledge helped focus our discussions to ensure their goals were aligned with mine.

When goals are achieved, celebrate! Acknowledge good work by showing gratitude for performance. In today's world, when we are so caught up in the work to be done, often we do not take the appropriate time to acknowledge successes.

Because people are human, you need to be prepared as a leader to handle significant failures appropriately. I certainly made my share of errors. Leadership failures can be devastating. Coaches can make a huge impact, both positive and negative, through how they handle people when bad things happen. Learn what happened, why, and help the leader recover.

Is the army's appraisal and development-support-form process perfect? Of course not. But when it was used, it helped guide leaders in their coaching efforts. When leaders failed to use it, its effectiveness eroded. The army process has stood the test of time; it has been hugely successful in providing the basis for army decisions on promotions, selections for schools, and future assignments.

One of the most powerful tools to help coach leaders and teams in the army is the after-action review, or AAR. The army AAR is the equivalent of what is commonly known as a hot-wash or debrief, versions of which have been going on for thousands of years. The AAR is conducted at all levels of the army, can be written or verbal, can be formal or informal, or as simple or complex as needed to achieve the desired results. Fundamentally, AARs help determine the results of decisions. They provide insights that highlight strengths and needs for immediate improvement focused on achieving greater results. The AAR typically takes place shortly after the event, while all details are still fresh in the minds of the participants. See Appendix E for much more detail on this valuable tool.

Being an effective listener enables a deeper understanding of what happened and why; more meaningful dialogue about complex problems surface. Listening, which is both a choice and a skill, takes practice to master and is critical for coaching.

I have worked for people who were magnificent listeners, and I have also worked for people who appeared to be deaf. Their words, tone of voice, and body language made it clear they had no clue what I was saying and clearly did not care.

There is art to speaking as well. The best coaches learn how to express thoughts, goals, and concerns freely, with clarity. When clear guidance is the order of the day, they double check to ensure their people heard what was said correctly. Effective coaches master the art of asking probing, insightful questions.

Face-to-face communication cannot be left out of any coaching experience. Respectful, recurring, regular face-to-face communication breaks down barriers, reduces anxiety, and builds trust. Much can be learned from spoken words, tone of voice, and especially from body language during in-person meetings. While it is natural and useful to take advantage of all the opportunities that technology offers, technology will never replace human contact for inspiration and encouragement.

Leaders must have the courage to address unsatisfactory performance. Not everyone will have the capability or aptitude to be successful in every endeavor. All too often, good people serving in leadership positions fear the task of confrontation. They don't want to hurt people's feelings or don't want to put at risk their own reputation of being a nice guy or gal. They hope something will magically happen which will turn an underperformer around and all will be well in the end.

Magic seldom happens.

Just as we expect physicians to correctly diagnose our health issues, leaders must correctly diagnose the reason for substandard performance. Start by understanding the intended outcome, then compare intentions with what actually happened. Was there a competence issue or a commitment issue? Was there a miscommunication? Were there resource shortfalls? The biggest mistake leaders make is never addressing the core issue.

There are many and significant consequences when people are not held accountable for their performance. Results are not achieved. Supervisors and others are forced to pick up the slack. When some good performers see no consequence for substandard performance, their own performance deteriorates. Integrity disappears. Discipline erodes. Morale evaporates. Leaders are not taken seriously. Problem employees become a cancer in the organization. The best people leave. Everyone watches to see if the leader takes corrective action.

Leaders who fail to take action to create positive change in underperformers (or remove them) are doing a great disservice to their institution.

Competent, dedicated people who do their best but fail at a task can be devastated by the experience. Coaches can make a huge impact, positive or negative, by how they handle their people in these situations. One of the most dramatic lessons of competitive sports is dealing with the downside; no one wins every contest. In sports, you learn how to get back up after being knocked down. I also had bosses who made my mistakes opportunities for me to learn. I embraced this approach and incorporated it formally in my own published leadership philosophy when I assumed new leadership roles in organizations; this is termed "underwriting mistakes in the pursuit of excellence."

Coaches should learn about themselves during the coaching process, too. It is not always easy to get feedback from subordinates, especially if there are potential consequences for criticizing a leader's performance. Be creative in how you solicit this important information. I made a habit of asking questions during exit interviews in the army, when soldiers depart for new assignments. Individual appraisals were completed, which helped alleviate the fears of potential consequences.

Four questions can be of great assistance in helping establish an open line of communication to achieve good feedback. When asked with genuine interest, people respond to these questions with more interest and honesty.

- What can I do for you?

- What do you think?

- What is on your mind?

- How am I making your life more difficult?

Marshall Goldsmith uses the term *feedforward* when asking others for input on how to change behaviors in the future. The whole idea of asking what can be done to be more effective in the future is an effective way to generate more acceptable, honest dialogue. Be creative. Discover ways to learn about yourself.

★ STORY ★

Giff Daughtridge, GM, Nucor Steel, Hertford, South Carolina

In 1999, Giff Daughtridge became the general manager of a new startup steel plate plant for Nucor Corporation in Hertford, North Carolina.

For the previous sixteen years, Daughtridge had served in various positions within the Nucor organization. He was a family man, married, with two kids. He was honored to be selected to lead this new plant. He embraced the Nucor culture: "We care about our teammates, our customers, the environment and the communities in which we live and work. It's not just our way of doing business; it's our nature."[35] Among his long list of exceptional leadership qualities, Daughtridge was passionate about caring for people, with a relentless focus on safety.

---

[35] "OUR CULTURE." Nucor Culture. Accessed March 13, 2019. https://nucor.com/our-culture.

Daughtridge was keenly aware of the criticality of his success in meeting the growing global demand for the steel products his plant was tasked to produce. Expectations were high: Hundreds of millions of dollars were on the line and the lives of 400 people were going to be changed forever. This was Nucor's first plate mill, so many of the processes and applications were new to the entire team.

Nucor Corporation is the largest steel producer in America, made up of over 20,000 people, with the mission to provide the highest quality, lowest cost steel products in the world. They are the largest recycler of any material in North America.

As the general manager of the startup plant, Daughtridge faced enormous challenges, from construction and equipping the facility to getting the right people on board to lead this effort. One of his most significant challenges was developing and aligning his team of leaders. Many of his leaders were going to endure the most stressful times of their lives. They were going to need Daughtridge's help, his support, his advice, and his counsel. Daughtridge in turn, was going to need their help ensuring he was doing all he could to enable their success. The core group making up the team came from a variety of backgrounds, mills, and experiences inside of Nucor and out.

Daughtridge recognized the fundamental need for establishing both a detailed set of expectations and an open line of communication. He met with his leaders individually and as a group on a regular basis. Goals for each leader were clearly identified. Issues, challenges, concerns, and solutions all got visibility quickly. Resources were allocated to ensure each leader had what he needed to be successful. Excellence was the named goal in all aspects of construction and personal development. A system of accountability was implemented through formal and informal performance assessments. Leadership mistakes became learning opportunities. There were no secrets; everything was discussed in the light of day. Daughtridge's relentless focus on caring for people and their safety earned him the respect and admiration of the entire division of 400 people.

This was not an overnight success story. There were struggles along the way, but Daughtridge's persistence and consistency in listening to his leaders and their people paid huge dividends. Team members were enthused about their work. Production exceeded standards. Personnel performance was exemplary. Safety was paramount. Five years after groundbreaking, the plate mill was Nucor's most profitable. Daughtridge attributes his focus on coaching as one of his most valuable keys to success.

In 2007, as a result of superior performance at Hertford, Daughtridge was selected to lead the largest plant in the Nucor company in Berkeley, South Carolina. In addition, all four of the department managers at the startup became general managers of their own plants. Four others who backfilled them went on to become general managers of their own plants. Daughtridge does not get credit for everything that happened at the Hertford plant, but he does get credit for being part of the team that achieved such enormous success.

The best coaches bring out the best in their people. They discover the unique gifts of their people, thank them for their good work, and show confidence in them. They ensure the tools and resources are made available to be successful. They encourage innovation and taking appropriate risks all in the pursuit of excellence. Underwriting honest mistakes will enhance their trust in you and confidence in their own capabilities. Your success as a coach will be measured by the success of your people.

Remember, effective one-on-one coaching can be the catalyst for attracting and retaining the best people who will ultimately help your organization achieve the desired results.

Leadership Tips—
Building Competence And Confidence

- **Establish a standard approach to coaching sessions.** Standardize how and when you engage your people in your one-on-one sessions. Tailor them as necessary to meet the specific needs of your people. Have a clear agenda regarding what needs to be discussed and how you plan to execute. Prepare for each session. Be consistent.

- **Establish goals and strategies to achieve.** Establish and achieve mutual agreement on goals. Ensure individual and team goals are aligned with the organization's goals. Collaborate on a strategy to achieve success. Gain insights into personal goals and aspirations.

- **Enforce accountability by assessing performance.** Consistently assess performance through periodic check-ins and meetings. Enforce standards by holding people accountable. Be positive in your attitude toward people. Inspire commitment to excellence. Be generous in showing gratitude. Address unsatisfactory performance. Underwrite honest mistakes in the pursuit of excellence. Seek feedback on your performance.

CHAPTER 7

Embrace Trusted Relationships

Bottom Line Up Front: Embrace trusted relationships by knowing and caring for your people, exercising humility, and spending quality time with your people outside of work.

Most people are not going to be successful in life's journey on their own. And when the going gets really tough, people will seek out those they trust to look for support and advice.

Many books have been written about the profound topic of trust. In this short chapter, I intend to highlight how vital trust is in building relationships to the army as well as the business world. I will share some best practices used in the army that can help business leaders build trust in their own worlds.

In one great book that addresses trust, *Five Dysfunctions of a Team*, author Pat Lencioni highlights, "Trust lies at the heart of a functioning, cohesive team. Without, teamwork is all but impossible."[36] What Lencioni says is absolutely true within the army, an organization built entirely of teams—thousands of them.

---

[36] Lencioni, Patrick. The Five Dysfunctions of a Team: Team Assessment. San Francisco, CA: Jossey-Bass, 2012.

Building relationships based on mutual trust trumps everything else when it comes to effective leadership. The army is made up of people, of human beings whose basic needs are no different than the needs of those not in uniform. Soldiers want to work for and with people they trust.

When trust is absent in military units, the consequences are significant, even catastrophic: decisions are questioned, commitment evaporates, discipline erodes, and units become ineffective, leading ultimately to mission failure. Many of these same consequences are equally important in business.

True leadership comes to life when mutual trust is established between leaders and followers. Trust is created when people understand each other and are willing to work together to achieve common goals. Leaders must create a culture in which people are not afraid to object, criticize, or ask for help. Building trust takes time—it must be earned. Losing trust takes only a flash. And once trust is lost, it takes a long time to recover.

Love and support grow among soldiers of all ranks who live life together, train together, and sacrifice together. Trust between soldiers is fundamental to achieving the camaraderie or *esprit-de-corps* found in the army and its sister services. You cannot command *esprit-de-corps*; you must cultivate and inspire it. Camaraderie grows with shared sweat and sacrifice as people train and live together. *Esprit-de-corps* is the secret sauce that helps build trust and distinguishes great teams from good teams.

As one advances up the ranks in the army or business world, trusting subordinate leaders with responsibility and authority to make decisions can be difficult. This is especially true for executives moving into new positions where relationships with direct reports did not exist prior. I believe in the saying, *"If you want to go fast, go it alone; if you want to go far, build the team."* Leaders who believe they can go it alone quickly find themselves not a good fit for most organizations.

The socialization process in the army is unique. Army units are constantly transitioning organizations, where units can turn over one-third of their organization each year. New soldiers arrive and depart every month, with the bulk of the transitions occurring in the summer months. Learning how to quickly build trust is a perpetual challenge for every leader and soldier.

In the business world, loss of trust is one of the most common reasons why people leave their place of employment. In the army, soldiers do not have many options due to their contractual commitment.

Being promoted in the army and continuously being assigned to positions of increased responsibility, trust takes on new dimensions. As an example, as a brigadier general in charge of a large staff in the Pentagon, I had many smart, professional people assigned to me. Together we were responsible for a host of significant, complex programs in support of the army. Decisions needed to be made all the time. I had to learn to trust my professional staff; they knew how the army staff operated, how the budget process worked, and many other aspects of the Pentagon environment that were new to me. My staff engaged me when they disagreed with my opinions, providing compelling rationales for their recommendations. Mutual trust enabled us to have engaging, professional, open discussions that ultimately led to better decisions.

Make no mistake; every part of the BRAVE guide contributes directly to building trust. While the army environment is unique in many ways, there are valuable lessons that can be learned to help build camaraderie in businesses. What follows here are three essential practices I learned while in the army that can help you cultivate trust with your people.

Know and Care for Your People

There is no more important time to show genuine care and empathy for people than when tragedy strikes. Memorial services are regularly scheduled for soldiers who have died on active duty. Soldiers from the unit attend funerals at the home of the fallen. The army assigns casualty assistance officers to help families navigate the challenges associated with their loss. A wide variety of family services are available to support families during deployments and other times of need. These are just a few of the many ways that the army takes care of its own.

I learned very early in my career that every soldier has a story. It was always enlightening to learn where soldiers came from, how they grew up, why they joined, why they stayed in the army. What I learned about soldiers could fill volumes. When leaders care enough to learn those stories, positive relationships begin to form.

I also remember when leaders sought to learn more about me and my family. I could tell when it was genuine and when it was not. Engagement opened up opportunities to connect, to establish a bond.

Army leaders demonstrate care for their troops in many ways. One way is to simply ask for input regarding an upcoming decision or issue. I vividly remember, as an army general, being asked often for my advice by other senior officers. I also remember as a young army lieutenant when my boss, a captain, asked me for my input on a significant challenge in the unit. I remember how these leaders made me *feel* when they valued my opinion. I also remember how many others never asked, never concerned themselves with what I could offer. It was important for me to realize that my opinion mattered.

There is great truth to the saying, "People do not care how much you know until they know how much you care." In the best units in which I served, I felt the love and support of those around me. I knew they would come to my aid if needed, just as I would for them. Trust is enhanced when people know they have each other's backs.

I knew the best minute of every day was the minute I spent with people. I learned the value of this precious time because of the overwhelming feedback I got during coaching sessions and exit interviews with departing soldiers. Soldiers shared with me how grateful they were when I cared enough to learn about them. The more senior I became, the happier soldiers were to see I was human, that I put my pants on one leg at a time, that I smiled, laughed, and made mistakes in my career.

Feedback can be a valuable tool to learn the truth about an organization, an issue, a potential crisis, or even a behavior challenge. It can help build trust. Feedback can also lead to loss of trust if leaders never ask for it, or fail to take action when it is clearly warranted.

There are times when trust is gained by confrontation with those who failed to perform to a standard. Also known as "tough love," this is a form of genuine caring, both for the individual who needs to be held accountable and other members of the team who are picking up the additional work. I had such a challenge in the summer of 1983. I had just taken over as the commander of the army company in South Korea. One of the most important relationships I was looking forward to was with my senior enlisted soldier, my battle buddy, whom I will call First Sergeant Baker (not his real name).

First Sergeant Baker had twenty-two years in the army, was a Vietnam veteran, and well qualified to be the senior sergeant in our company. Shortly after I assumed command, I attended the company softball game where I witnessed First Sergeant Baker being drunk, laughing, and socializing with all his junior soldiers in the stands. What would be the impact to the organization if this behavior was allowed to continue? If soldiers believed that behavior was acceptable, then they would engage in what I would characterize as *misplaced trust*. I had an immediate decision to make—fire or correct the behavior and give a second chance. The other leaders were watching me.

The next morning, I met with First Sergeant Baker in my office. I shared my disappointment in and the impact of his behavior that I witnessed the previous day at the softball game. There was a lengthy period of silence before he responded. He opened up his heart, apologized profusely, and acknowledged that he had made a terrible mistake. He knew he had lost my trust and confidence in him while earning the misplaced trust of his soldiers. He understood the profound impact on the organization and the troops if he did not take immediate action to change. He appealed for a second chance to prove himself worthy of his position. I granted that request.

First Sergeant Baker lived up to his pledge. He never took another drink of alcohol for the rest of his tour of duty in Korea. He apologized to all the soldiers and rebuilt his relationships with the other officers and senior sergeants in the organization. He recommitted himself to the development of his troops. His life changed forever that day. Our company grew in its success, accomplishing every mission thrown our way, in large measure to the leadership of First Sergeant Baker. He turned out to be a magnificent leader, enforcer of standards, embracer of outstanding performance, and truly loved his troops. We spent considerable time together over the months. He earned back my trust. I learned several years later that he had been promoted to the next higher grade, sergeant major, the highest rank for an enlisted soldier. He had never consumed another drop of alcohol for the rest of his career.

I learned from this experience the importance of giving people a second chance. I needed to be respectful of his career of outstanding service and that he needed help—my help. That experience would affect my decisions the rest of my career as a soldier and leader.

Exercise Humility

Humility is not complicated. But it also is not easy for many. Leaders with humility recognize they may not have all the right answers. They set aside their egos. They are effective listeners who seek the truth. They genuinely want to grow as leaders and do all they can to help others do the same.

I heard someone once refer to being humble as using a window-mirror approach to life. When things go well, look out the window to find those who deserve the credit. When things go bad, look in the mirror to see who needs to take the blame.

It is empowering to organizations when the boss admits mistakes or acknowledges that he does not have all the answers. I feared making mistakes and I also had difficulty asking for help. Those are not good combinations of weaknesses. In either case, I always admired leaders who shared their vulnerability. I began modeling their behavior and it helped me overcome, to some degree, my own challenges.

Toxic leadership can be a challenge, either in the army or in any organization. Toxic leaders are those who have egos bigger than a house. They take credit for everything good and blame others when things go bad. They do not tolerate mistakes, micromanage everything, and take no interest in the knowledge and skills of their people. They create horrible organizational climates where the morale of soldiers or employees is destroyed. Trust is nonexistent.

Spend Quality Time With Your People Outside Of Work

Social customs and traditions are monumentally important to the army culture. Formal occasions and celebrations of important holidays events are attended by soldiers of all ranks, along with their spouses or significant others. These events create times to pause and reflect on the profession, show gratitude to those deserving, and continue to build trust among the people. They help build teams, generate camaraderie that can help morale, and bring joy to the organization. They provide opportunities for many of the junior folks to actually meet and have a face-to-face conversation with leadership. They demonstrate a priority by willingness to invest time and resources in events away from the stresses of daily work.

Because soldiers transition every two to three years, team-building remains a constant priority. Welcoming newly arriving officers and saying farewell to those departing are favored traditions in the army. These events are very informal, take place in civilian clothes, usually include dinner, and always include spouses or significant others. At these events, new folks are introduced for all to meet. For those departing, the sharing of stories gets things started, followed by appreciation for their many accomplishments, and the event ends with a presentation of a farewell gift. The principle purpose of all such gatherings is to help build relationships.

I remember how good I felt being invited into the homes of senior officers. As I grew up, I hosted many informal social events in my own home. I always took an interest in hosting events for my key leaders to help build the bond among the leadership team upon whom I depended so heavily. There is something to be said about inviting others literally into your living room. They see how you live; the family pictures on the mantel, the books on your shelves, the kids toys in the corner, the dog bowls in the kitchen. For many, these events expose that the senior leader is actually human. These events enabled people to relax, get to know each other, and laugh at all the stupid things we did. They helped relieve stress. At the very least, these events taught us to recognize how serious our jobs were, but not to take *ourselves* so seriously.

You will know you have achieved the goal of a trusting relationship when you can see it in people's eyes and feel the spirit of cohesion.

$ Specials $
⇨ CARE FOR YOUR PEOPLE
⇨ EXERCISE HUMILITY
⇨ QUALITY TIME OUTSIDE OF WORK

EMBRACE TRUSTED RELATIONSHIPS

★ STORY ★

Roslyn Marshall, Senior Nurse Manager, AU Health at Augusta University, Augusta, Georgia

Roslyn Marshall is a registered nurse and currently a senior nurse manager for the Augusta University Medical Center.

Embracing trusting family relationships has been Roslyn Marshall's motto since she was a little girl. She was the oldest of three children who lost both parents while a teenager. Living with her grandparents, who already had ten children of their own, it became clear to her that relationships were the key to survival.

Four years after graduating from nursing school, she had already been promoted to the position of a nurse manager in the medical center. After three years of success in one manager position, she was asked to manage a nursing unit that was experiencing enormous challenges and suffering from high turnover, high nurse vacancy rates, poor patient experience scores, and low morale.

After some serious soul searching, she decided to embrace the challenges of managing this nursing unit. The challenges were many. To achieve success, Marshall knew she had to develop trust with her staff, the physicians, and ultimately the patients.

"Tearing Down the Walls" became the unofficial motto of the team. Her initial task was to get to know all of her people. Information sharing came next, including clarification of standards of performance. These two elements set the foundation for breaking down the barriers that were undermining the team's potential for success.

One member of the team was unable to adjust to the new culture of care, despite considerable coaching. Roslyn had the courage to engage this nurse and help her find reassignment to a different position more suitable for her talents. When the other members of the team witnessed this important decision, their trust in Marshall was reinforced.

On another occasion, a younger member of her staff recommended a different approach to team meetings. Initially, Roslyn did not accept the recommendation, as it was different from what she had learned over many years. When Roslyn's way was struggling with success, she reluctantly consented to try the younger nurse's idea. It did not take long for Roslyn to see the wisdom of this nurse's recommendation, as it produced far more productive results than her old way. She graciously apologized to the entire team for letting her ego get in the way of what was best for the unit. This was trust-building in action.

Over time, effective team collaboration emerged, providing cohesive services to meet the needs of patients and their families. Trust became the hallmark for Roslyn's relationships with her staff and the physicians. After eighteen months, a culture of staff pride and ownership was established. Patient satisfaction grew, staff vacancy was eliminated, the turnover rate was reduced, and most of all, quality patient care increased dramatically.

Roslyn attributes building trusted relationships, one person at a time, to being one of the key elements of the successful culture transformation.

Leadership Tips— ### Building Competence And Confidence

- **Know and care for your people**. Engage your people often, wherever you can. Learn about them and their families. Advocate for their welfare. Treat all fairly. Be a dependable source of information and action. Seek and listen to feedback. Attend funerals. Provide comfort and support to those in need.

- **Exercise Humility.** Be humble. Let go of your ego. Give credit to all those who work for you when things go well. Take blame when things go wrong. Admit when you make mistakes. Do not be afraid to apologize when appropriate.

- **Spend quality time with your people outside of work.** Create opportunities for joy by spending quality time with your people and their families outside the normal work environment. Find ways to welcome the new folks and appropriate ways to bid farewell to those departing. Help people learn about you and your family.

SECTION III

★

The Value Of BRAVE Cultures

CHAPTER 8

Strategic Cultures

It was July 8, 1974. Sweat was dripping off my face as I got off the bus that fateful morning on the campus of the US Military Academy in New York. I was with a bunch of other nervous guys who had all spent a sleepless night in a New York City hotel in anticipation of reporting for our first day at West Point. I was met by the "Man in the Red Sash," an upperclassman from the academy wearing a red sash around his waist distinguishing him as a man of authority. I do not recall his exact words that day, but I was profoundly introduced to the culture of the West Point. Haircut, uniform, and a new disciplined way of life would be my future for the next four years.

The word culture conjures up a wide variety of thoughts. From my own experience, at its core are the values and expected behaviors that contribute to the unique environment of an organization. These values are the glue that binds people together. Culture is more than values, however. Culture also includes shared attitudes, customs, written and unwritten rules, how the organization does business, and how it treats its employees and customers. Culture is a significant foundational element of any organization.

I learned at West Point and my time in the army that the burden was on me to adjust to the organization's culture, not the other way around.

The US Army Strategic Culture

The US Army is big, with well over one million soldiers in the active, reserve, and national guard components. The army developed its culture over many, many decades. The strategic army culture is shaped by a host of decisions and practices defined at the highest levels of the army. These items govern how the army operates as an enterprise. The culture of the army is unique. It is different from all other organizations and even other military services. Specific elements that help define the army culture include oaths, creeds, values, codes of conduct, uniforms, doctrine, education and training, discipline, chain of command, standard operating procedures, family support, performance-based promotions, length of tours of duty, and more.

The role of senior leaders in establishing a winning culture cannot be overstated. Leaders cannot leave culture to chance and assume that all members of the organization get it.

The most significant change in overall army culture in my generation was the establishment of all-volunteer force in 1973. The impact to the army was dramatic. Big changes were necessary if this experiment was going to be successful. According to a 2006 study by RAND Corporation, four components critical to success were identified: attention and leadership from the top, comprehensive analysis of job performance versus cost, the need to attract recruits, and investment of financial resources.[37]

The army took extraordinary measures to address all four elements highlighted by the RAND study, and more. There have been challenges along the way, but the all-volunteer force remains a vital and successful element of our nation's security.

---

[37] Rostker, Bernard. "The Evolution of the All-Volunteer Force." RAND Corporation. Last modified August 28, 2006. Accessed February 22, 2019. https://www.rand.org/pubs/research_briefs/RB9195.html.

The change in culture did not happen overnight. On the contrary, it took years and remains a work in progress. The army had to learn how to attract and recruit qualified people. The challenges associated with recruiting new soldiers are vast, and the success achieved by the army is a testament to how the army adapts to meet the needs of society as well as the army.

The army also had to learn how best to retain quality people as it built a professional force. It did so through training and developing leaders, combined with providing opportunities for professional advancement in an expansive set of possible career fields.

One of the most dramatic changes was the creation of the professional noncommissioned officer corps—the sergeants—who are rightfully referred to as the "backbone of the US Army." Sergeants are the leaders who grow up from enlisting as privates. To help attract and retain these experienced soldiers, the army had to determine appropriate pay, allowances, and health care support, along with other incentives like education opportunities through the GI Bill.

One of the next big refinements to army culture was the formal establishment of seven core values (described in detail in chapter 3). The army has always been focused on ethics, leadership, and the profession of arms, but took a dramatic step in clarifying what character means when it formally established these values. The army continues to adapt its culture to address the changes in our society's social, economic, and technological realities.

BRAVE Leaders Contribute To Building Winning Strategic Cultures

Business leaders of large organizations can learn from the army's approach to developing and sustaining a winning culture. The BRAVE foundation captures many of the significant elements that can help with that process.

Consider using BRAVE as a starting point for assessing the health of your organization's culture. Take action to address the most important gaps highlighted by the assessment.

One technique I found valuable in helping guide my personal behaviors as a senior leader in the army was the development of my top ten. I wanted to discipline myself in executing. I captured these elements on a 3 × 5 index card, laminated to protect from weather. I carried it with me all the time and referred to it often. The list was compiled from a host of mentors whose advice to me I treasured. I still have the card.

Leadership

1. Before speaking: Think, breathe, ask "Is it worth it?"
2. Find 'em doing something right
3. Best minute—one invested in people
4. Simplify the complex
5. Guidance: Positive, focus on priorities
6. Keep sense of humor—smile
7. MBWA—Have a positive purpose
8. Embrace those in need
9. Tell 'em thanks—overt and often
10. Be strong, confident—esp. in the toughest times

★ STORY ★

Bob McDonald: Strategic Culture At Procter & Gamble Company And Veterans Affairs

One of the most profound examples of creating a winning strategic culture was at Procter and Gamble Company (P&G). For many, many decades P&G has been a leader in the global consumer goods industry. There are many reasons for the company's long-term success, but the fundamentals are core values and investment in development of leaders, according to Bob McDonald, the retired chairman, president and CEO of the company from 2009 to 2013.

McDonald was a West Point graduate and spent five years in the army before joining P&G in 1980. He rose through the P&G ranks, serving in many different positions across the globe. Results are one of the first metrics used to evaluate success. Over McDonald's tenure as CEO, P&G's stock went from $51.10 to $81.64, a 60 percent increase. P&G was in large measure by McDonald's design, one of the fifteen most valuable companies in the world by market capitalization.[38]

These results were achieved for a number of reasons. Two of them, McDonald will tell you, were tireless focus on core values and developing leaders. P&G's core values include integrity, leadership, ownership, passion for winning, and trust.[39] All of these were essential to creating an inclusive workplace that attracts, develops, and retains the best talent. In 2007, McDonald was the chief operating officer and was asked to build a general manager college where individuals were taught values-based leadership, a curriculum that McDonald created. As the COO, McDonald himself trained hundreds of leaders. In 2009, when McDonald become the CEO, he continued to train the company's leaders and also took values-based leadership to a new level.

In 2012, P&G ranked number one in *Chief Executive*'s list of top forty companies for leaders. McDonald genuinely believed the

---

[38] Moss Kanter, Rosabeth, and Marcus Millen. "Still Leading (B1): Hon. Bob McDonald-Profiting from Purpose." Harvard Business Review. October 21, 2017. Accessed February 22, 2019. https://hbr.org/product/still-leading-b1-hon-bob-mcdonald-profiting-from-purpose/318050-PDF-ENG.

[39] "Our Purpose, Values and Principles." Procter & Gamble. 2018. Accessed December 20, 2018. https://www.pg.com/citizenship2018/index.html#/Ethics-Responsibility

leader development program was a necessity if P&G was going to have the leaders it needed to be successful over time. That belief led to a significant investment of time and money; P&G created the 5E leadership model described in chapter 7. This model was developed by a team of outstanding P&G leaders including A. G. Lafley, McDonald's predecessor as CEO, and Ron Taff, who was a leadership trainer in the company.

Unlike other leadership models, P&G's leadership program and trainers focused on the behaviors necessary to exhibit leadership. They inculcated those behaviors into all aspects of the culture of the company: criteria for hiring, performance appraisals, vocabulary of leadership, and more. They even capitalized on a web-based survey that could be used to evaluate one's leadership in 360 degrees.

Experiential learning for many of the company's leaders through periodic transfers abroad enabled P&G to focus on expanding its cadre of knowledgeable global leaders.

Trust was at the very foundation of everything that happened at P&G. As an example, a first-name basis of address was common at the company, even for the senior leaders. This was a surprise to McDonald, coming from the army where no one called their superior officers by their first name. This first-name basis was simply part of the company culture and emblematic of the value of trust. The creation of a more open environment helped break down barriers of communication, which in turn helped the exchange of ideas and recommendations, and ultimately helped build trust.

McDonald retired from P&G in 2013, and in 2014 he was selected as the eighth secretary of the US Department of Veterans Affairs (VA). The VA organization was in a period of crisis after the previous secretary resigned. He quickly assessed that the strategic culture was at stake for the VA. It had to change. And it was not going to be easy. "It starts with purpose, values and principles, which is to me the bedrock of every organization," said McDonald.

He developed his initial strategy, called The Road to Veterans Day, which included three main points: 1) rebuild trust, 2) improve metrics, shorter wait times, people getting care, and 3) put together long-range programs that would lead to a fundamental transformation.[40]

The employees at the VA were living and operating in a fear-based culture rather than a principle-based culture. This fear was manifested in the constant visibility of bad decisions highlighted by media scrutiny. And as a result, leaders were not going to stray from the letter of the law.[41] To rebuild trust with veterans, employees, and key stakeholders, McDonald and his leadership team had to get to the heart and soul of this organization by the establishment of core values and commitment to the inspired development of leaders.

He brought many successful fundamentals of growing a strategic culture from P&G to the VA. First was to establish and inculcate a set of core values. These values would serve as foundational building blocks for reestablishing trust among the workforce. These evolved into Integrity, Commitment, Advocacy, Respect, and Excellence (ICARE), and they truly define who the VA is. These values drive the behaviors of staff across VA. He had to ensure that every VA employee understood his or her critical role to support the VA's

[40] Buell, Ryan W, Robert S. Huckman, and Sam Travers. "Improving Access at VA." Harvard Business Review. November 4, 2016. Accessed February 22, 2019 https://hbr.org/product/improving-access-at-va/617012-PDF-ENG.

[41] Ibid.

commitment to care for and serve our veterans, their families, and beneficiaries.[42]

Another technique McDonald instituted to help overcome the bureaucracy of a rigid government agency was a "Call me Bob" campaign, just like the first-name basis that was commonplace at P&G. In addition to traveling to sites to interact with veterans, staff, and stakeholders, he wanted information (especially bad information) to travel up to leadership quickly. The intimacy of personal relationships would facilitate this.

From a leader development perspective, McDonald launched a training program called Leaders Developing Leaders (LDL). LDL began with 300 of the VA's most senior leaders, including McDonald and his deputy Sloan Gibson, coming together for an intensive two-day session on leadership and values. McDonald and Gibson did much of the training themselves. Following that initial session, LDL cascaded throughout the organization as senior managers who attended the initial session were tasked with facilitating new LDL training for their subordinate leaders.

By 2015, LDL had cascaded through the ranks to the point that 1,500 VA leaders had received the training. Gibson noted that "a medical center director came up to me after (LDL) and said I'm finally prepared to go out and take some risk because I feel like if I do the right thing, according to our values, the right thing for veterans and taxpayers, it will be okay."[43]

---

[42] "Learn to Communicate Assertively at Work." Veterans Employment Toolkit Handout. December 17, 2013. Accessed February 22, 2019. https://www.va.gov/vetsinworkplace/docs/em_eap_assertive.html

[43] Buell, Ryan W, Robert S. Huckman, and Sam Travers. "Improving Access at VA." Harvard Business Review. November 4, 2016. Accessed February 22, 2019. https://hbr.org/product/improving-access-at-va/617012-PDF-ENG.

One module of LDL titled "Veterans Experience" specifically focused on imbuing a spirit of principles-based leadership. The team goal was to have 12,000 additional employees go through the training by 2016.

The clear message was a significant investment in developing leaders from the executive team down to every manager in the organization. The program was targeted toward the goals of the company.

The strategic culture established by McDonald and his leadership team was profound. The two key initiatives just described along with his five separate, comprehensive strategies helped the organization achieve many victories in a short period of time and set the VA on a course for achieving and sustaining a high level of performance. Evidence of this significant change in performance across the enterprise is a comprehensive set of metrics that clearly demonstrated positive results, ultimately improving care to veterans and their families. It is interesting to note that two dozen veterans' organizations asked the new administration to keep leadership in place at VA despite the presidential transition; in 2016, however, a new administration arrived in Washington, DC, and with it a new secretary of the VA assumed the helm.

McDonald clearly understood and embraced the importance of establishing a strategic culture through developing leaders of character, putting leadership development programs in place that help build competence and confidence in his leaders across the organization. He left a formidable legacy at the Procter and Gamble Company as well as at the VA.

When I think of Bob McDonald in his role at P&G and the VA, I am reminded of the Rudyard Kipling poem "If." My father gave me a framed version of this poem when I was a young army officer, and I have kept it close at hand ever since. Of particular note are the words: "If you can talk with crowds and keep your virtue or walk with kings—nor lose the common touch...you'll be a man my son."[44]

---

[44] Kipling, Rudyard. Rewards and Fairies / Rudyard Kipling. London: Macmillan, 1915, c1910., n.d.

CHAPTER 9

Boots-On-The-Ground Cultures

After graduating from the military academy, I arrived at my first army unit at Fort Bragg, North Carolina. The first three people I met were my immediate boss (the company commander, a captain), my senior boss (the battalion commander, a lieutenant colonel), and the senior enlisted soldier in the unit (the command sergeant major). All three seasoned military leaders were to become key influencers in my new life. In those three short meetings, I was introduced to the organizational culture of the unit in which I would serve over the next three years.

I am referring to this culture as "boots-on-the-ground," or subculture of a much bigger organization.

The idea of small-unit culture highlights the fact there is a distinct difference between the *big* organization culture, or strategic culture, and the culture where people actually work on a daily basis. But they are intimately related. For small to medium size companies, there is only one culture.

The US Army Boots-On-The-Ground Culture

The battalion size unit in the army is perhaps the best example of where a subculture of a large organization like the army comes to life. A typical battalion has 750 soldiers and is led by its commanding officer, a lieutenant colonel with eighteen years of service. A battalion has its own history, lineage and honors, its own flag, and its own distinguished unit crest. It is a close-knit organization that trains together, deploys together, and lives together.

The commander of the battalion has the obligation to ensure each subordinate leader understands and embraces the mission and values of the organization and extends that influence over the rest of the unit. In addition to meeting the intent of *big* army with regard to culture, the battalion commander is expected to bring to life his own personality and style to his organization. As an example, while the big army at the corporate level defines its seven values with abundant clarity, how well they are lived and brought to life at the lower levels is the responsibility of the local commander. While the big army establishes policy and guidelines on how to support families, how well that intent is executed at lower levels is up to the local leaders. One of the powerful attributes of the army is the concept of leaders leading their own way, capitalizing on their strengths, learning from their mistakes, and perpetually growing. The same principles hold true for business leaders.

The next level of command below the battalion is the company with 100-200 soldiers. Below the company is platoon, with 30-50 soldiers. Each of these levels has their own sub-culture based on their leadership.

There is a very truthful saying in the army that units take on the personality of the commander. If the local commander is an engaging, positive, inspirational leader, chances are the other leaders are going to model that attitude and behavior. On the other hand, if the local commander is a micromanager, a screamer, responds irrationally to bad news, enforces a no-defects environment, then the subordinate leaders are likely to model that behavior as well.

One valuable way I learned how to determine if my philosophy and priorities were being transmitted down the chain of command was engaging the troops themselves. This technique is commonly referred to as MBWA, or management by walking around. There is always something to be learned from spending time with the troops. I typically had a main purpose in my walks. I would focus on training goals, deployment issues, saying thanks, or seeking out soldiers for a unique purpose. In these engagements, I inevitably learned about important issues that merited action. Every once in a while, I needed some inspiration myself and sought soldiers (unbeknownst to them) to remind me of how privileged I was to serve with them.

Handling crises or tragedies is always a test of character for those in charge. Successfully navigating through the turbulent waters that crises bring can also be an uplifting experience for the organization. The best leaders anticipate crises and prevent where possible some from occurring. However, crises cannot all be anticipated or prevented. Preparation for such events will pay great dividends for leaders.

To help commanders establish and sustain positive work environments, the army requires surveys to be conducted early in a new commander's tour of duty and annually thereafter. The army calls them "command climate" surveys. They are done at battalion and company level. The focus is to learn the truth of how effectively the organization is functioning. A variety of areas are addressed: leadership, unit readiness and cohesion, training, morale, concern for families, respect, discrimination, diversity, and more. These surveys are comprehensive. The results are shared with the commander's supervisor to ensure visibility and follow-up actions are addressed.

While initially skeptical about these surveys, I learned over time how valuable the assessments were. Their importance to me peaked when I was in the position of commander. These assessments were critical in helping to learn the truth, and even the perceptions, about critical areas that affected the effectiveness of the organization. They exposed blind spots that I and other leaders needed to see. They taught me the gift of feedback reinforcing the need to listen to the voices of the troops.

They also taught me how critical it was to take action, where needed, to address the challenges that were exposed.

Commanding officers in the army are solely responsible for establishing an environment within their organization that cultivates trust, discipline, respect, and genuine care for the welfare of the troops. Staff principals at senior levels in the army have the same responsibility for their people.

Toxic Leadership Environments

Unfortunately, the army is not immune to toxic leadership. Nor is any business. I have worked in environments where army leaders exhibited toxic behaviors that led to dissention in the ranks. While the army takes extraordinary care in the selection of its senior leaders, there is no fail-safe mechanism that prevents leaders from becoming abusive or toxic.

The impacts on organizations suffering from a toxic environment can be devastating. In the army, soldiers can seek assistance outside their organization. These include the inspector general and the Equal Opportunity office. But soldiers are contractually bound to the army and cannot simply choose to leave. In a business environment people have more freedom to simply depart, but that is not always an easy decision to make. The real challenge is how to enlighten the leadership to know there are serious problems within the organization so that corrective action can take place and those who reported it are safe from retribution.

Senior leaders in any organization, army or business, have the absolute obligation to know when abusive or toxic conditions exist in their organizations and to take action to correct the problem. When this obligation is neglected, the organization is destined to suffer.

BRAVE Leaders Contribute To Building Winning Business Boots-On-The-Ground Cultures

The best leaders in the business world, just as in the army, understand the importance of tireless pursuit to maximize organizational effectiveness. Just as in strategic cultures, the BRAVE foundation captures many of the significant elements that can help build and sustain a winning boots-on-the-ground culture for the business world.

Developing a winning culture does not happen overnight—it takes time and deliberate effort, especially by senior leadership. Just like in the army, everyone in a business organization is a keeper of the culture, but its most significant influencer is the number one person in charge. For example, consider the mega company Walmart. Sam Walton, the original owner of Walmart, hired Don Soderquist in 1988 to be his Chief Operating Officer. Sam led by example and expected Soderquist to be his "keeper of the culture." In a personal interview, Soderquist highlighted the reason Walmart continued to reach unprecedented levels of success long after the passing of Mr. Walton: The winning culture that was instituted and kept alive by leaders across the organization.[45]

Maintaining the intent of the strategic culture was one thing, but how well it was implemented in the stores around the country was another. Soderquist used to travel to meet the leaders and employees of these stores with the clear intent to determine if the strategic culture envisioned by Sam Walton was implemented properly, kept alive and well down in the trenches (so to speak).

Just like in the army, employees of companies tend to take on the personality of their leader. Employees are much more inclined to adhere to core values if the leadership does. And they are just as likely to ignore core values if the leadership also ignores them.

---

[45] Blanchard, Kenneth. Leadership by the Book-Twelve Candid Interviews on Leadership. DVD. United States: Pacific Media Ministry, 2004.

Wise business leaders invest in some method of measuring employee satisfaction or engagement, such as a survey. When administered professionally, much can be learned from surveys about team members and what needs to happen to strengthen the organization. If toxic conditions exist, there will likely be higher turnover rates and other indicators of employee dissatisfaction. When mutual trust exists between the leaders at the local level and their team members, conditions are ripe for achieving high levels of success.

⋆ STORY ⋆

Jeff Annis, Cofounder, Advanced Services, Inc.

Jeff Annis is the visionary cofounder of Advanced Services, Inc., a company providing residential pest and termite management primarily in the Augusta, Georgia area. He grew the business from a one-person start-up in 1986 to forty-six team members with annual gross sales of more than $5 million by 2018. While his success was based on a number of criteria, he shared with me that he attributes his most significant contributions to establishing a culture of learning. In Jeff's words:

> "We view leadership development to be as important as growing sales, marketing and revenue. We persistently attend leadership conferences, bring in great workshop leaders and hold in-house training. In our culture, we always stress core values such as continual improvement and loyalty. When you develop great people in their leadership capability, they feel more loyal to the team because they see investment being made in their futures. Otherwise, it would not have been possible to grow to one of the top 30 single location pest management operations in the USA."

Outsiders recognize the exceptional quality of the Advanced team development program, as Advanced was awarded the Atlanta region and the National Best and Brightest Places to Work For designation in 2018.[46]

Consider using the BRAVE foundation to assess the health of your organization's culture (see Appendix A). Take action to address the most important gaps highlighted by the assessment.

---

[46] "Introducing the Winners - Atlanta's 2018 Best and Brightest Companies To Work For*." The Best and Brightest. Accessed March 13, 2019. https://thebestandbrightest.com/events/2018-best-brightest-companies-work-nation/winners/?winyear=356.

CHAPTER 10

Your Leadership Legacy And Looking To The Future

Imagine you have just departed your position as a senior leader in an organization in which you were proud to serve. You committed a substantial portion of your life to this organization. How do you want to be remembered after you are gone?

This was a profound question asked of me while attending a special leadership program preparing me for my assignment as the commanding officer of an army battalion. I never stopped thinking about that question and, more importantly, how critical it was for me to get the response right.

We are all leaving a legacy. There is no escaping it. You are building your legacy now. How will your people act after you are gone? How will people remember you? The real question is, will yours be a positive legacy or something else?

Once you define what you want your legacy to be, the next step is determining how you are going to achieve it. Your legacy is derived from what you truly believe in, those values that you hold in your heart and soul. What do you believe is your purpose in life? As a leader, you must believe you can make a better difference in the lives of others.

It does not make any difference how old or young you are. You still have the opportunity to change the lives of people, to encourage them, to help them grow.

In the early fall of 1974, I was immersed in academics and playing football at West Point when I received a book in the mail from a wonderful mentor of mine from high school, Hank Kleinfeldt. The book was titled *So Run Your Race*.[47] Using a sports analogy, the principle message from this book was to identify the spiritual strength required to commit to your sport, which required full coordination of body, mind, and spirit. Kleinfeldt knew I would need that strength to achieve success at the academy, in the army, and in life after. Part of my legacy would be forever to remain steadfast in my race to the finish line.

Twenty years later, in 1994, I took command of an army battalion of 750 soldiers. With command comes the enormous challenge of being responsible for everything that happens or fails to happen in the organization. I had to develop my very first personal leadership philosophy, which would help guide me as the leader of this unit.

For those who have never visited the Galleria dell'Accademia in Florence, Italy, I would encourage you to consider a trip. It is the home of many masterpieces in the world of art, especially those of Michelangelo. When you walk down the long outdoor corridor toward the location where the famous statue of David stands in its wonder, there are many others of what appear to be partially completed sculptures of Carrara marble carved by Michelangelo.

In many ways, I see myself in these sculptures from a leadership perspective. For instance, I know I have some refined leadership skills represented by portions of the sculpture that are smoothly polished. I also have some leadership skills that are a bit rough around the edges,

[47] Neal, Patsy. *So Run Your Race: An Athlete's View of God*. Grand Rapids, MI: Zondervan Publishing House, 1974.

just as they are depicted in the rougher parts of the carving. And I know I have some skills I have yet to discover, just like the portions of sculpture that have not been carved at all. Part of my legacy is clearly that I am still learning and growing. I remain a work in progress.

While I did not realize what servant leadership was until late in my military career, I believe I have always sought to be a servant-leader. At its core, servant leadership to me is selfless service. It begins in the heart. It is a genuine commitment to serving a cause greater than oneself. It is about helping others be successful. Once you, as a leader, set the vision and direction for an organization, the servant-leadership approach then causes you to focus doing all you can to help others achieve their own goals, which contribute to that vision and mission.

In May of 1999, I had the honor of meeting Major General Perry Smith, US Air Force (retired). Perry is a 1956 West Point graduate, fighter pilot, speaker and an author. He was our guest speaker at National Defense University. At the end of his great presentation, he offered his assistance to anyone in the audience of 300.

I was a colonel at the time, getting ready to assume command of a brigade (3,500 soldiers) at Fort Bragg in two months. I took him up on his offer and he was gracious in providing me some great advice. Over the years I learned that Perry has many gifts. One element of his legacy is his tireless efforts to help others grow. Perry has been one of the most influential mentors in my life. He invited me to coauthor an updated version of *Rules & Tools for Leaders* in 2013, which was the catalyst that propelled me to formally launch my own leadership coaching company.[48]

---

[48] Smith, Perry M., and Jeffrey W. Foley. *Rules & Tools for Leaders: from Developing Your Own Skills to Running Organizations of Any Size, Practical Advice for Leaders at All Levels.* Penguin Group, 2013.

My Legacy

- I want to be remembered as a BRAVE leader.

- I want to be a leader of character.

- I am in perpetual pursuit of learning leadership competencies.

- I have committed the second half of my life to help develop leaders, for which BRAVE sets the foundation.

- I want to be the most effective leadership coach possible.

- I am tireless in pursuit of building trusted relationships through-out my professional and personal life.

Looking To The Future

I challenge you to consider BRAVE as your guide to grow yourself and those you lead.

A profound day in our recent military history merits sharing, as it exemplifies one of the most important elements of exceptional leadership: the retention of quality men and women in the force.

The date was July 4, 2008. Our nation had been at war for more than seven years. The location was Camp Victory, the United States military headquarters in Baghdad, Iraq. On that day, 1,215 soldiers, sailors, airmen, and marines raised their right hands, pledging to continue defending the land of the free. This was the largest reenlistment ceremony since the all-volunteer military had been established in July 1973.

Why did so many troops choose to remain in uniform, and to do so in the combat theater where so many had deployed multiple times with enormous sacrifices of their families, through more than seven years of constant conflict in Afghanistan and Iraq? I believe leaders of all ranks serving their troops in extraordinary ways was a principal contributor.

And when you sacrifice and suffer in defense of America, you learn to love it more.

I wish you the best in your leadership journey.

APPENDIX A

Assessment For Developing BRAVE Leaders

To achieve positive and lasting results in any leadership behavior, you must commit yourself to a four-step process. The process begins with an assessment, followed by the creation of an action plan based on the priorities discovered in the assessment. Plans are no good unless they are rigorously executed. Finally, a sustainment strategy is developed that reinforces the learning and includes updates on the assessment and new action plans.

Use the assessment template below to help determine where you are on each of the five components of the BRAVE guide. It can also be used to evaluate others.

Place an X on the scale below that corresponds to the total for each of the five elements (minimum score is 3, max is 15). Once your assessment is complete, determine what is most important for you and your organization. Create the action plan and execute.

	3	**6**	**9**	**12**	**15**
B					
R					
A					
V					
E					

1. Be a Leader of Character

- **Discover yourself.** Be a leader of honesty and integrity. Determine what you are good at by assessing your strengths. Discover what you enjoy doing. Learn what you stand for. Learn what motivates you. Use this knowledge to help guide your everyday actions, how you interact with others, and understand where you can best contribute. Help others learn how to be most effective in communicating with you.

  POOR 1 _____ 2 _____ 3 _____ 4 _____ 5 _____ GREAT

- **Establish and communicate core values.** Ensure you and your organization have established core values that truly represent what is most important. Ensure the behaviors are well defined for each value. Be tireless in your communication of the values until everyone gets it.

  POOR 1 _____ 2 _____ 3 _____ 4 _____ 5 _____ GREAT

- **Live the values.** Lead by example every day through living the values. Make decisions based on values and share the process with all. Ensure the leaders from executive level down to first-line supervisors commit to them. Routinely recognize those people who demonstrate living the values.

  POOR 1 _____ 2 _____ 3 _____ 4 _____ 5 _____ GREAT

  TOTAL: _____

2. Reveal and Reinforce Leader Competencies

- **Identify Core Competencies.** Clearly identify the key competencies that every individual member of the organization needs to learn.

  POOR 1 _____ 2 _____ 3 _____ 4 _____ 5 _____ GREAT

- **Identify Leader Competencies.** Clearly identify the most important leader competencies that must be learned by managers at all levels, including the executive leaders.

  POOR 1 _____ 2 _____ 3 _____ 4 _____ 5 _____ GREAT

- **Make Competencies Visible.** Inspire growth by bringing these competencies to life. Clearly document them in employee handbooks. Integrate them into the performance appraisal system. Highlight them during regular scheduled coaching sessions and group meetings.

  POOR 1 _____ 2 _____ 3 _____ 4 _____ 5 _____ GREAT

  TOTAL: _____

3. Attack with a Leader Development Program

- **Determine the Goals of Your Leader Development Program.** Use the company's vision, mission, and business objectives as the foundation for establishing goals. Perform comprehensive assessments on the individuals' leader competencies that highlight gaps in skills needed to accomplish the mission. Based on your assessments, derive goals for the program, document them in writing, and share them with all.

  POOR 1 _____ 2 _____ 3 _____ 4 _____ 5 _____ GREAT

- **Determine How You Will Accomplish the Goals**. Determine the best combination of training & education, experiential learning and coaching to achieve the goals. Use standard development tools to help create repeatable processes to maximize learning. Consider tailored programs for high-potential performers and those selected for promotion into critical leadership positions.

  POOR 1 _____ *2* _____ *3* _____ *4* _____ *5* _____ *GREAT*

- **Execute and Sustain the Program.** Execute the program. Reassess periodically to ensure the program is meeting its goals and enhancing performance of leaders and the organization. Sustain your program by committing resources in the future to achieve a culture of learning.

  POOR 1 _____ *2* _____ *3* _____ *4* _____ *5* _____ *GREAT*

  TOTAL: _____

4. Value Coaching Excellence

- **Establish a standard approach to your coaching sessions**. Standardize how and when you engage your people in your one-on-one sessions. Tailor them as necessary to meet the specific needs of your people. Have a clear agenda regarding what needs to be discussed and how you plan to execute. Prepare for each session. Be consistent.

  POOR 1 _____ *2* _____ *3* _____ *4* _____ *5* _____ *GREAT*

- **Establish agreed-upon goals and strategies to achieve.** Establish and achieve mutual agreement on goals. Ensure individual and team goals are aligned with the organization's goals. Collaborate on a strategy to achieve success. Gain insights into personal goals and aspirations.

POOR 1 _____ *2* _____ *3* _____ *4* _____ *5* _____ *GREAT*

- **Enforce Accountability by assessing performance**. Consistently assess performance through periodic check-ins and meetings. Enforce standards by holding people accountable. Be positive in your attitude toward people. Inspire commitment to excellence. Be generous in showing gratitude. Address unsatisfactory performance. Underwrite honest mistakes in the pursuit of excellence. Seek feedback on your performance.

POOR 1 _____ *2* _____ *3* _____ *4* _____ *5* _____ *GREAT*

TOTAL: _____

5. Embrace Trusted Relationships

- **Know and care for your people.** Engage your people often, wherever you can. Learn about them and their families. Advocate for their welfare. Treat all fairly. Be a dependable source of information and action. Seek and listen to their feedback. Attend funerals. Provide comfort and support to those in need.

POOR 1 _____ *2* _____ *3* _____ *4* _____ *5* _____ *GREAT*

- **Exercise humility.** Be humble. Let go of your ego. Give credit to all those who work for you when things go well. Take responsibility and blame when things go wrong. Admit when you make mistakes. Do not be afraid to apologize when appropriate.

POOR 1 _____ *2* _____ *3* _____ *4* _____ *5* _____ *GREAT*

- **Spend quality time with your people outside of work.** Create opportunities for joy by spending quality time with your people and their families outside the normal work environment. Find ways to welcome the new folks and appropriate ways to bid farewell to those departing. Help people learn about you and your family.

POOR 1 _____ *2* _____ *3* _____ *4* _____ *5* _____ *GREAT*

TOTAL: _____

APPENDIX B

Boy Scouts Of America *Scout Oath* And *Scout Law*

Scout Oath

On my honor I will do my best to do my duty to God and my country and to obey the Scout Law; to help other people at all times; to keep myself physically strong, mentally awake, and morally straight.

Scout Law

The Scout Law has twelve points. Each is a goal for every Scout. A Scout tries to live up to the Law every day. It is not always easy to do, but a Scout always tries.

A Scout Is:

- **Trustworthy.** Tell the truth and keep promises. People can depend on you.

- **Loyal.** Show that you care about your family, friends, Scout leaders, school, and country.

- **Helpful.** Volunteer to help others without expecting a reward.

- **Friendly.** Be a friend to everyone, even people who are very different from you.

- **Courteous.** Be polite to everyone and always use good manners.

- **Kind.** Treat others as you want to be treated. Never harm or kill any living thing without good reason.

- **Obedient.** Follow the rules of your family, school, and pack. Obey the laws of your community and country.

- **Cheerful.** Look for the bright side of life. Cheerfully do tasks that come your way. Try to help others be happy.

- **Thrifty.** Work to pay your own way. Try not to be wasteful. Use time, food, supplies, and natural resources wisely.

- **Brave.** Face difficult situations even when you feel afraid. Do what you think is right despite what others might be doing or saying.

- **Clean.** Keep your body and mind fit. Help keep your home and community clean.

- **Reverent.** Be reverent toward God. Be faithful in your religious duties. Respect the beliefs of others.[49]

---

[49] "The Foundation of Scouting," Boy Scouts of America, https://www.scouting.org

APPENDIX C

United States Army *Seven Core Values*

Core Values

Loyalty

Bear true faith and allegiance to the U.S. Constitution, the Army, your unit and other Soldiers. Bearing true faith and allegiance is a matter of believing in and devoting yourself to something or someone. A loyal Soldier is one who supports the leadership and stands up for fellow Soldiers. By wearing the uniform of the U.S. Army you are expressing your loyalty. And by doing your share, you show your loyalty to your unit.

Duty

Fulfill your obligations. Doing your duty means more than carrying out your assigned tasks. Duty means being able to accomplish tasks as part of a team. The work of the U.S. Army is a complex combination of missions, tasks and responsibilities—all in constant motion. Our work entails building one assignment onto another. You fulfill your obligations as a part of your unit every time you resist the temptation to take "shortcuts" that might undermine the integrity of the final product.

Respect

Treat people as they should be treated. In the Soldier's Code, we pledge to "treat others with dignity and respect while expecting others to do the same." Respect is what allows us to appreciate the best in other people.

Respect is trusting that all people have done their jobs and fulfilled their duty. And self-respect is a vital ingredient with the Army value of respect, which results from knowing you have put forth your best effort. The Army is one team and each of us has something to contribute.

Selfless Service

Put the welfare of the nation, the Army and your subordinates before your own. Selfless service is larger than just one person. In serving your country, you are doing your duty loyally without thought of recognition or gain. The basic building block of selfless service is the commitment of each team member to go a little further, endure a little longer, and look a little closer to see how he or she can add to the effort.

Honor

Live up to Army values. The nation's highest military award is The Medal of Honor. This award goes to Soldiers who make honor a matter of daily living—Soldiers who develop the habit of being honorable and solidify that habit with every value choice they make. Honor is a matter of carrying out, acting, and living the values of respect, duty, loyalty, selfless service, integrity and personal courage in everything you do.

Integrity

Do what's right, legally and morally. Integrity is a quality you develop by adhering to moral principles. It requires that you do and say nothing that deceives others. As your integrity grows, so does the trust others place in you. The more choices you make based on integrity, the more this highly prized value will affect your relationships with family and friends, and, finally, the fundamental acceptance of yourself.

Personal Courage

Face fear, danger or adversity (physical or moral). Personal courage has long been associated with our Army. With physical courage, it is a matter of enduring physical duress and at times risking personal safety. Facing moral fear or adversity may be a long, slow process of continuing forward on the right path, especially if taking those actions is not popular with others. You can build your personal courage by daily standing up for and acting upon the things that you know are honorable. [50]

---

[50] "United States Army Seven Core Values." www.army.mil. Accessed August 13, 2018. https://www.army.mil/values/.

APPENDIX D

Sample Action Plan

Effective leaders at all levels take action. They don't just think about what they should do—they act. Below is a simple example of an action plan, with many other templates on the internet. The message is to use this template as a tool to help generate action, holding yourself and others accountable. The actions can be part of a larger leader development plan with measurable actions or deliverables directly tied to performance goals. The list can also be those essential actions that contribute to changing a specific behavior or leadership skill.

Name:	Date:

The Goal, Objective, or Behavior:

#	Action Step	Obstacles	Resources Available	Date for Completion
1				
2				
3				
4				

APPENDIX E

The After-Action Review

The After-Action Review, or AAR, is one of the most powerful tools used by the military and business world to help develop leaders and teams, ultimately to help achieve greater results. The AAR described here is adapted from the US Army.[51]

The AAR is conducted at all levels of any organization, can be written or verbal, can be formal or informal, or as simple or complex as needed to achieve the desired results. In its simplest form, four questions are addressed by all who participated in the actual planning or execution of an event.

The After-Action Review (AAR) template:

1. What did we set out to do?

2. What actually happened?

3. Why did it happen?

4. What are we going to do next time?

As an example, AARs are used with a small team of six soldiers seeking to achieve certification in their crew drills only if it can accomplish a set of specific tasks to an established standard within a designated period of time. The team would conduct the training event. After time expires, an immediate AAR would be conducted with the evaluator and entire team to learn what went well and what needed to change, if anything. Candid discussion is encouraged by all. If the team did not meet the certification standard, they would retrain, then reconduct the certification event with intent of getting it right the second time. An AAR would follow the second time as well, with a new decision regarding certification or more training. AARs used in this fashion are exceptional in helping to gain proficiency in team performance.

On a bigger scale, as a commander in charge of a battalion of 750 troops, I hosted AARs after every major field exercise. We would announce the date for the AAR in advance, along with related details or primary topics to focus. The same basic template was used, many leaders and participants provided their own feedback on the questions, and action plans were put into place to ensure we learned from our experiences.

On a much bigger scale, army divisions and corps commanded by generals conducted AARs after major training events, with senior commanders and staff leading their portions of the event. Even at the Department of the Army level AARs are conducted. For example AARs for disaster relief operations occurred that included many agencies inside and outside of the government as there were always significant lessons to be learned.

AARs are common place in the business world, especially those businesses that are keen on improving their results and developing their people. They are used to discover goodness or challenges. Examples include hiring or firing actions, safety incidents, medical surgeries, clinical procedures, emergency action procedures, project completions, major sales actions, proposal wins or losses, acquisitions and mergers, reorganization efforts, new initiative reviews, annual conferences, and much more.

AARs are most valuable when they are embraced by the leadership and become standard development tools used throughout the organization. They also can be used to evaluate significant events experienced by other organizations serving as great case studies or vignettes for you to learn.

APPENDIX F

Military Decision-Making Process— For Business

There is an art and science to mastering the skill of decision making. The science includes measurable criteria such as cost, production or delivery rates, and time. The art includes the more ambiguous elements such as complexity, impact of leadership, intuition, the competition, or the environment. Mastery of the skill of making good decisions comes with a good process and lots of practice.

The army's Military Decision Making Process (MDMP) is "an iterative planning methodology to understand the situation and mission, develop a course of action, and produce an operation plan or order."[52] When this process is applied to a business, it allows the manager and the planning staff the ability to critically analyze a problem or task and develop the way ahead to solve that problem. This process can be applied to situations as simple as what office furniture to buy, to much more complex decisions such as how to best grow the company or to divest a major product or service. This decision-making process can be as rigid or flexible as the person in charge requires. Based on time constraints, one can abbreviate or eliminate steps, or if time is not a factor, one can remain committed to all steps.

---

[52] U.S. Army, Army Doctrine Publication *ADP 5-0, The Operations Process*. May 2012, Headquarters, Department of the Army, Washington, DC, Pg. 8

This MDMP consists of seven steps that are: receive the mission, mission analysis, course of action (COA) development, COA analysis, COA comparison, CAO approval, and orders production. Roughly translating these terms into their business equivalent, they become: problem statement, information gathering, design the options, weighing the options, comparing the options, the decision, and communicating the decision.

Army-toCivilian MDMP Terminology Comparison

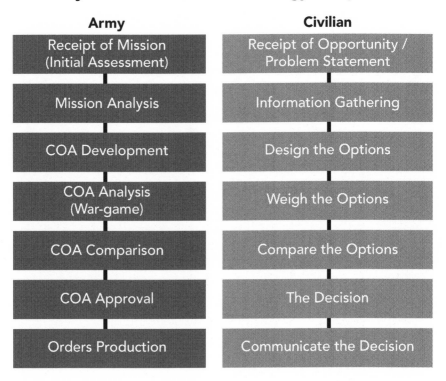

Army	Civilian
Receipt of Mission (Initial Assessment)	Receipt of Opportunity / Problem Statement
Mission Analysis	Information Gathering
COA Development	Design the Options
COA Analysis (War-game)	Weigh the Options
COA Comparison	Compare the Options
COA Approval	The Decision
Orders Production	Communicate the Decision

Below are brief descriptions of each step adapted from the army's process for business.

1. Problem Statement

A business leader must define the problem to solve or address. Defining the problem is often the hardest task in the process. The lack of precision in this opening step can plague an organization. Problems can be phrased in the form of a question or more of a mission statement. They can focus on a "yes/no" option or a "what is the best way to…" which demands multiple options for consideration. Many problem statements also contain an explanation of the reasoning process to help people understand the rationale for even considering the task. Example problem statements include:

- Should we acquire company ABC to help grow our business throughout the region?

- What is the best way to expand our product line to meet the needs of today's consumers?

- Should we expand our headquarters to include a human resources department because of the extensive growth of the company?

- Should we continue to install, operate and maintain our IT infrastructure or outsource?

- What product or service should we divest ourselves of in order to meet anticipated budget reductions?

- What is the best way to increase the efficient usage of our surgical operating rooms to reduce patient scheduling backlog?

2. Information Gathering

Once the problem is well understood, information gathering becomes the next critical task. The manager, along with the staff, conducts a thorough analysis to better understand the situation. This analysis identifies *what* must be accomplished, *when* and *where* it's done, and, most importantly *why*. If specific resources are not available within the organization, then this process helps determine what is needed for resolution.

Categorizing the information gathered is often best organized into the subsets below:

- *Facts.* Information known to be true and that is applicable to solving the problem.

- *Assumptions.* Suppositions assumed to be true that are required to continue planning, based on relevant facts, which bear upon solving the problem. Ideally, assumptions should be validated or invalidated throughout the process.

- *Risk.* The possibility of losing something of value as planning continues; managers must often assume some level of risk when solving a problem.

- *Constraints.* A restriction, identified in the problem statement, that limits or inhibits the manager or staff trying to solve the problem.

- *Tasks.* When assessing the specific work to be done that is embedded in the problem statement, it is helpful to understand what the show-stopper tasks are (things that will derail the solution if not considered), the specifically called-out tasks that must be accomplished, and other implied tasks that merit acknowledging and must be done to solve the problem. Not all problem statements or missions have all of these, but it is helpful to be sure to capture them if they do exist.

- *Resources Available.* Personnel, equipment, money, transportation, etc. that are available to the team and address a potential solution.

As information is gathered by both staff and the manager, they should formulate a cohesive assessment and begin to identify potential design options. Be cautious. If during information gathering one gets too far ahead or wedded to a particular potential outcome, the team may invalidate their own analysis or lose sight of their original problems.

3. Design the Options

Simply put, a design option is a broad solution to an identified problem. As the manager and staff develop design options, they should consider more than one way to solve the problem. Each option designed is a separate and distinct way to solve the problem. To collaboratively build the design options the manager and staff use the tasks from the problem statement in step 1, information gathered and analyzed in step 2, any further guidance from the upper-level management, and any specialized skills from the staff sections. Thus, each potential solution must meet five criteria: feasible (viable), suitable (fitting), acceptable (appropriate), distinguishable (unique), and complete (comprehensive).

While each design option may not fully identify all potential variables to solve the problem, the options should be as complete as possible in order to compare them against each other.

4. Analyze Each Option

A set of evaluation criteria needs to be developed to determine how each option will be assessed. These criteria serve as the "gauntlet" each option will be run through and are derived from the five categories of criteria listed above: feasibility (viability, such as cost), suitability (fit, such as *consistent with the culture of the organization or customer environment*), acceptability (appropriateness, such as *amenable to leadership or stakeholders*), distinguishability (uniqueness), and completeness (comprehensiveness, such as *does it address the entire problem*). Perform a rehearsal of the option, recording the pros and cons based on the evaluation criteria. Often, a table is established with a clear metric recording the results of analysis. Examples are:

- 1, 0 or -1, with 1 being the most advantageous

- 1, 2, 3, with a positive number being the most advantageous

- +, 0, -, with + being the most advantageous

In the development of criteria, there may be one that has increased importance over others, which would dictate adding weight to that criteria of 2X or more. It is important to remain objective and not allow personal preference to interfere with what the staff *thinks* the boss wants. Avoid premature conclusions; be persistent and impassionate. Avoid comparing design options to one another, as that's the next step.

5. Compare the Options

Once the team completes assessing each individual option, then the manager and staff must compare them. When the results of each assessment are included in the same table, often one option stands out as the best when you add up the scores. It is during this comparison stage that engaging dialogue and feedback becomes critically important to ensure all the known aspects of the options are understood. Based on the comparison, a recommendation emerges.

6. The Decision

The recommendation for a decision is derived from the results of the comparison of all options. Typically, the decision-maker is presented with each option, the results of the analysis, with a recommended solution. This is another opportunity for the group to discuss all aspects of the options and recommendation. There are times when no option is decided upon, a different option that was not recommended is chosen, or even a hybrid solution that would best benefit the company is chosen.

7. Communicate the Decision

Once the decision is made, how that decision is communicated throughout the organization is determined. This final step bridges the gap between planning and preparation. The staff makes any possible updates management required following the decision and begins writing the actual document that solves the identified problem. All details relevant to the decision are addressed clearly and openly communicated to all parties involved.

Businesses, much like the military, survive and thrive through effective, proven processes. While detailed, thorough, resourced, and complete planning can make or break an organization, it must be acknowledged that some flexibility should be anticipated. There is an old axiom in the army that states, "No plan survives first contact with the enemy; the enemy has a vote." The "enemy" in the civilian world is competition and the unknown.

APPENDIX G

Recommended Reading

One of the most valuable ways to learn how to be more effective in our ability to lead others is through reading. Learning how others, especially experts, achieved success can be found in many, many books. What is learned through reading must then be put into practice. Authors of the books become mentors and coaches, even though we may never meet or communicate with them directly. The books below are some of my absolute favorites written by experts in leadership. I added some notes about each book that will help clarify what "golden nuggets" resonated with me. Pick a book from among these or choose another favorite. But read and act. What you learn from your own investment in reading may be the real game changer in your life!

What Got You Here Won't Get You There (Marshall Goldsmith, 2007). Marshall Goldsmith is one of America's top executive coaches. This best-selling book highlights valuable insights that can have an immediate impact on leaders. Implementing his suggestions changes behaviors in ways that will help you perform at a higher level. From his decades of coaching top executives throughout the world, he identifies twenty leadership behaviors that you should consider starting, stopping, or improving. That list merits your review. He also introduces the concept of "feed-forward," a fascinating approach to focus change in behavior for the future. This book helped me in every leadership job I have had, and still does.

Leading at a Higher Level: Blanchard on Leadership and Creating High Performing Organizations, Third Edition (Ken Blanchard and colleagues, 2018). This is a comprehensive summary of what I consider the "best of" forty years of great work by Ken and the Ken Blanchard Companies. It presents the definitive discussion about using SLII—the most widely used leadership model in the world—to lead yourself, individuals, teams, and entire organizations. I have benefitted tremendously over many years by the extraordinary content in this book.

The Leadership Challenge (James Kouzes, Barry Posner, fifth edition, 2012). This is a perennial bestseller and one of the most comprehensive books on leadership I have read. Over thirty years of documented research is captured to help the reader understand the complex world of what it takes to be effective in leading others. It identifies the top leadership behaviors most important for leaders to learn. With the accompanying assessment tools, it can help diagnose strengths and weaknesses in the most important leadership skills. Included is a profound list of actions that coaches can take to have an immediate impact on the behaviors of their people. A wonderful book and guide for leaders at all levels.

The Five Dysfunctions of a Team (Patrick Lencioni, 2002). Patrick Lencioni provides an analytical approach illustrating that successful teams cannot be built and managed alone. The book is a fable wherein all principles of the book come to life through the story. Bottom line: Leaders need to build vulnerability-based trust with their people to achieve high-performing teams. As you progress through the book, the five dysfunctions are exposed, with actionable steps to address each. I have used this book in my own organization and shared its wisdom with many others. A great read for leaders at all levels, especially those leading or those who desire to lead teams.

Leading Change (John P. Kotter, 1996). This is an exceptional book on leading change in organizations by a world-class expert. It is inspiring and educational. The eight-stage process highlighted here is profound in its advice on how to execute a successful change process. It will help leaders at all levels including those who must initiate change along with those who must embrace and implement.

The Effective Executive (Peter Drucker, 2006) This foremost leadership expert, author, and management practitioner has written over thirty books; many are bestsellers. Eight powerful, proven practices of effective executives are described in detail. The measure of the executive, Drucker reminds us, is the ability to "get the right things done." Exceptional guidance by the master for anyone desiring to excel in the executive role.

How to Win Friends and Influence People (Dale Carnegie, 1936). Though written in 1936, this book remains a classic on leadership. It provides wonderful ways to positively influence people. Carnegie emphasizes that "leaders must have a deep, driving desire to learn, and a vigorous determination to increase their ability to deal with people." The book is full of stories that highlight best practices of leadership. He encourages the reader to choose one, act on it, then adjust as you grow and learn. While some of the material is dated, many of the principles remain as valid today as they were in the past. An excellent read.

The Secret: What Great Leaders Know—and Do (Ken Blanchard, Mark Miller, 2014). The framework provided in this story is universally applicable to people of all ages, at all levels of responsibility, from parents to new employees to senior executives. This book is a fable that provides a great stage for learning leadership principles. The story captures the challenges of a new supervisor in her leadership role and how she overcomes them with sage advice from her mentor. This book remains one of my all-time favorites and it is where I was initially introduced to the concept of servant leadership.

Wooden on Leadership (John Wooden and Steve Jamison, 2005). This is an extraordinary book that captures the legendary UCLA basketball coach's lessons on leadership from forty-one years of coaching. His goal as a coach was always to get maximum effort and peak performance from each of his players in the manner that best served the team. He never focused on winning and losing; rather, he emphasized giving your absolute best. Long-term, authentic leadership seeks to motivate people from the inside, through an appeal to the head and the heart, not by use of command and coercion. The "Wooden Pyramid of Success" is described in detail. I was most impressed by Coach Wooden's unwavering commitment to building character, demonstrating integrity, and focusing on values. Wonderful lessons from the competitive sports world for leaders in any profession.

Servant Leadership in Action (edited by Ken Blanchard and Renee Broadwell, 2018). This book is an incredible collection of essays contributed by forty-five leaders across all industries who share their inspiring stories about servant leadership. The book is organized into six different parts and includes basic principles, lessons learned, profiles of classic servant leaders, and firsthand accounts of effective servant leadership in action. The depth and range of this collection makes it one of the most definitive resources available on this powerful concept of leadership.

Rules & Tools for Leaders, 4th Edition (Perry M. Smith and Jeffrey W. Foley, 2013). I used previous editions of this book extensively in my leader development programs for years and had the honor of contributing to its revision. It is a comprehensive guide that provides practical advice in a host of areas for leaders at all levels, in all types of organizations, and in personal life. This book will help you grow as a leader from developing your own individual skills, to building teams, to running large organizations. Various editions are used in corporations, nonprofits, churches, military professional colleges, and leadership programs in schools from high school to MBA and executive MBA programs. It is a refreshing update with many new and revised chapters covering the breadth of leadership responsibilities.

ACKNOWLEDGMENTS

Hundreds of people have contributed to the successes I have been blessed with in my life. The list begins with my father and extends to Boy Scout leaders, teachers, and coaches in my early years. As I progressed up through the ranks of the military, the list grew rapidly to include soldiers of all ranks, civilians, colleagues and many, many friends. A whole group of other great people have had a positive impact on my growth after my retirement from the army. These lists are far too long to include here, but know that I value and appreciate all. I want to especially thank the people below for significant contributions to this focused effort.

Henry DeVries was my inspiration to write this book. He was also a marvelous coach, editor, and great mentor during this entire process. Devin DeVries, Denise Montgomery, Joni McPherson and the wonderful team at Indie Books International were wonderful in their support throughout the entire process.

Perry Smith has been a monumental mentor for me for many years and helped guide me in my life after the army.

Ken and Margie Blanchard have been inspirational mentors for many years, and I am enormously grateful to both. I have also grown as a leader, coach, and consultant because of the enormously talented team of people at Ken Blanchard Companies.

Bob McDonald, Chris Hughes, Ron Thigpen, Jeff Bevis, Jeff Rowe, Giff Daughtridge, Roslyn Marshall, and Jeff Annis were all kind enough to share their compelling leadership stories.

Those who made valuable contributions in many unique ways include: Robert Caslen, James Blanchard, Jerry DeMuro, Herman Bulls, David Hess, Pat Williams, Dina Dwyer-Owens, Bob Buford, Marshall Goldsmith, Jim Felton, Derek Thexton, Bill Zipp, Mick Ukleja, Dean Minuto, Brock Brown, Brent and Kelly Mallek, Frank Wagner, Angela Kegler, Phyllis Hennesy Hendry, Mark LeBlanc, Paul Menig, Michael Hauge, Patricia Fripp, Jim Horan, Toni Nell, Judy Carter, Denny McGuyer, Scott McChrystal, and Doug Thorton.

From a military perspective, those who were gracious enough to invest time helping me clarify my thoughts include: Thom Tuckey, Pete Farrell, Glenn Kennedy, Tom Faust, Bryan Ellis, Everett Greenwood, Lee Fullerton, Jim Toth, and Tom Clark.

Others who provided valuable insights include: Monty Hopkins, Drew Sanders, Virginia Foley, Bill Gibbs, Dan Albo, John Orth, Doug Lind, Steve Lee, Rick Toole, Lou Imbrogno, Richard Eyre, Craig Combest, Shawn Vincent, Brian Tidwell, Anthony Williams, Vera Stewart, Rich Henderson, John Martin, Darryl Leach, LaVerne Gold, Laurie Orth, Ed Presnell, Mike Uhle, Jay Forrester, Rick Franza, Wendy Verkade, Dave Brunk, Zach Kelehear, Mac Barnhardt, Gail Love, Fran Nunan, Clint Bryant, Roger Sublett, Chris Hansen, and Len Carlson.

I am grateful to Bill Woods for graphic illustrations and Luisa O'Connor for the photography.

Any omission of people who helped is entirely my fault, and I apologize. Know that I remain grateful to all.

A special thanks to my wife Beth, for her love, advice, incredible support, patience and understanding of the lost days, nights and weekends during this extraordinary journey.

ABOUT THE AUTHOR

Jeffrey W. Foley hails from Cincinnati, Ohio, graduated from West Point in 1978, and retired from the US Army as a brigadier general.

He runs a leadership development company called Loral Mountain Solutions. As an executive coach, he helps successful leaders get even better by achieving positive, lasting changes in behavior for themselves and the people they lead. As a speaker, he conducts presentations to companies and professional organizations around the country on how to build competent, confident leaders capable of leading high performing teams.

As a result of his work, his clients often share they have *more competence and confidence* in their leadership role, *more focus* on what matters, and have *more influence* with the people they lead.

He coauthored *Rules & Tools for Leaders* (4th edition, 2013), a down-to-earth, practical guide for leaders. He is a contributing author to a collection of essays in the book *Servant Leadership in Action* (edited by Ken Blanchard and Renee Broadwell, 2018).

He is a certified Marshall Goldsmith *Stakeholder Centered Coach*—one of the most unique and powerful coaching methodologies in the world. He is channel partner with the Ken Blanchard Companies, a partner with the Wiley Corporation (*Five Behaviors of a Cohesive Team, Everything DiSC)*, and a Certified Master One Page Business Plan Consultant with Jim Horan's *One Page Business Plan*.

He served over thirty-two years in the US Army, leading soldiers in war and peace. Throughout his military career, he served in leadership positions around the world, in constantly changing environments, all the time focused on the accomplishment of the mission and taking care of people.

Upon completion of military service, he spent two and one-half years as an executive administrator with Augusta State University and later Georgia Regents University & Health System.

Foley played intercollegiate sports at West Point and was an Eagle Scout. He was honored by his high school alma mater, Mariemont High, as both a Distinguished Alum and member of the Athletic Hall of Fame. He holds master's degrees in computer systems and National Security Policy, and an Honorary Doctorate of Humane Letters from Union Institute and University. He resides in Augusta, Georgia, and serves on four local and national boards. He remains a lifetime Cincinnati sports fan. The most significant award he received as a soldier was the opportunity to serve his country.

WORKS CITED

"100 Best Companies to Work For." *Fortune*. Accessed December 11, 2018. http://fortune.com/best-companies/.

"About Everything DiSC: Theory and History." John Wiley and Sons, Inc. Accessed February 22, 2019. https://www.everythingdisc. com/EverythingDiSC/media/SiteFiles/Assets/History/ Everything-DiSC-resources-aboutdisc.pdf.

A Leader's Guide to After-Action Reviews. Training Circular 25-20. Headquarters, Department of the Army, Washington, DC., 30 September 1993. Accessed February 24, 2019. http://www. au.af.mil/au/awc/awcgate/army/tc_25-20/tc25-20.pdf.

Beck, Randall, and Jim Harter. "Why Great Managers Are So Rare." Gallup.com. March 25, 2014. Accessed December 07, 2018. https://news.gallup.com/businessjournal/167975/why-great-managers-rare.aspx.

Blanchard, Kenneth. *Leadership by the Book-Twelve Candid Interviews on Leadership*. DVD. United States: Pacific Media Ministry, 2004.

Blanchard, Kenneth. "Leading at a Higher Level: Blanchard on How to Be a High-performing Leader." *Financial Times* Prentice Hall, 2010.

Carucci, Ron A., and Eric C. Hansen. "Rising to Power: The Journey of Exceptional Executives." Navalent, 2014. http://www. navalent.com.

Deloitte Touche Tohmatsu Limited. "The 2016 Deloitte Millennial Survey: Winning Over the Next Generation of Leaders." Deloitte.com. Accessed February 24, 2019. https://www2. deloitte.com/content/dam/Deloitte/global/Documents/ About-Deloitte/gx-millenial-survey-2016-exec-summary.pdf.

"Do CEOs with Military Experience Outperform Others?" ChiefExecutive.net. May 31, 2012. Accessed June 16, 2017. https:// chiefexecutive.net/do-ceos-with-military-experience-outperform-others__trashed/.

Espinoza, Chip, and Mick Ukleja. *Managing the Millennials: Discover the Core Competencies for Managing Today.* John Wiley & Sons, 2016.

"OUR CULTURE." Nucor Culture. Accessed March 13, 2019. https://nucor.com/our-culture.

Fisman, Ray. "CEOs Who Served in the Military Are More Honest. But They Make Their Companies Less Money." *Slate Magazine.* May 25, 2012. Accessed December 11, 2018. https://slate. com/business/2012/05/ceos-who-served-in-the-military-are-they-more-honest.html.

Fundamentals of Senior-level Leadership in Peace and War: P913: Advance Sheet Booklet. Fort Leavenworth, KS: U.S. Army Command and General Staff College, 1989.

Goldsmith, Marshall. *What Got You Here Won't Get You There.* New York: Hachette Books, 2007.

Human Capital Institute. "How to Accelerate Leadership Development." UNC Kenan-Flagler Business School. 2014. Accessed February 19, 2019. https://www.kenan-flagler.unc.edu/~/media/Files/documents/executive-development/unc-webcast-accelerate-leadership-development-deck.pdf.

Huckman, Robert S., Sam Travers, and Ryan W. Buell. "Improving Access at VA." *Harvard Business Review.* November 4, 2016. https://hbr.org/product/improving-access-at-va/617012-PDF-ENG.

Hughes, Christopher P. *War on Two Fronts: An infantry Commander's War in Iraq and Afghanistan*, Casemate Publishers, Philadelphia, PA, 2007, p.103-114.

"Introducing the Winners - Atlanta's 2018 Best and Brightest Companies To Work For®." The Best and Brightest. Accessed March 13, 2019. https://thebestandbrightest.com/events/2018-best-brightest-companies-work-nation/winners/?winyear=356.

Kipling, Rudyard. *Rewards and Fairies/Rudyard Kipling.* London: Macmillan, 1915, c1910., n.d.

Kotter, John P. *Leading Change.* Boston, MA: Harvard Business Review Press, 2012.

Labuda, Patryk I. "Lieber Code." Oxford Public International Law. September 2014. Accessed June 7, 2017. opil.ouplaw.com/view/10.1093/law:epil/9780199231690/law-9780199231690-e2126.

"Learn to Communicate Assertively at Work." *Veterans Employment Toolkit Handout.* December 17, 2013. Accessed February 22, 2019. https://www.va.gov/vetsinworkplace/docs/em_eap_assertive.html.

Lencioni, Patrick. *The Five Dysfunctions of a Team: Team Assessment.* San Francisco, CA: Jossey-Bass, 2012.

Moss Kanter, Rosabeth, and Marcus Millen. "Still Leading (B1): Hon. Bob McDonald-Profiting from Purpose." *Harvard Business Review.* October 21, 2017. Accessed February 22, 2019. https://hbr.org/product/still-leading-b1-hon-bob-mcdonald-profiting-from-purpose/318050-PDF-ENG.

Neal, Patsy. *So Run Your Race: An Athlete's View of God.* Grand Rapids, MI: Zondervan Publishing House, 1974.

"Our Purpose, Values and Principles." Procter & Gamble. 2003. Accessed December 20, 2018. https://www.pg.com/translations/pvp_pdf/english_PVP.pdf.

"Procter & Gamble Voted Top Company For Leadership Development | Newsroom." Russell Reynolds Associates. Accessed December 17, 2018. http://www.russellreynolds.com/newsroom/procter-gamble-voted-top-company-for-leadership-development.

Ray, Rebecca L. "For CEOs, It's Still About Developing Leaders: Strategy Is Nothing Without Effective Leaders to Execute." Development Dimensions International. 2018. Accessed February 19, 2019. https://www.ddiworld.com/DDI/media/trend-research/glf2018/global-leadership-forecast-2018_au-nz_leaders-at-the-core.pdf.

Reimer, Dennis J., and James Jay Carafano. *Soldiers Are Our Credentials: The Collected Works and Selected Papers of the Thirty-third Chief of Staff, United States Army.* Washington, D.C.: Center of Military History, US Army, 2000 Accessed February 24, 2019. https://history.army.mil/html/books/070/70-69-1/index.html/.

Rowe, Jeffrey A. *Just Do These Few Things: How to Find and Develop Exceptional Talent, Share the Wealth, and Build a Great Company and Culture*. Nunan Vogel Rowe, LLC, 2016.

Smith, Perry M., and Jeffrey W. Foley. *Rules & Tools for Leaders: from Developing Your Own Skills to Running Organizations of Any Size, Practical Advice for Leaders at All Levels*. TarcherPerigee, 2013.

Sorely, Lewis. A Better War: the Unexamined Victories and Final Tragedy of America's Last Years in Vietnam. Orlando: Harvest Book, 1999.

"The Foundation of Scouting." Boy Scouts of America, Accessed February 23, 2019. https://www.scouting.org.

"The West Point Leader Development System Handbook," published by the West Point Leader Development System Committee, United States Military Academy, West Point NY, May 2015.

Thorn, Chantal. "3 (Not So Secret) Secrets to Designing Effective Leadership Development Programs." D2L.com. Accessed Dec 16, 2017. https://www.d2l.com/enterprise/blog/3-not-secret-secrets-designing-effective-leadership-development-programs/.

U. S. Army Field Manual 22-100, Army Leadership, Headquarters, Dept of the Army, 1999.

U. S. Army Field Manual 6-22: Army Leadership. Headquarters, Dept. of the Army, 2006.

U.S. Army, Army Doctrine Publication *ADP 5-0, The Operations Process*. May 2012. Headquarters, Department of the Army, Washington, DC.

U. S. Army Field Manual 101-5, Staff Organization and Operations. Headquarters Department of the Army, May 31,1997. Accessed February 24, 2019. http://www.militaryfieldmanuals. net/manuals/staff_organization_and_operations

U.S. Military Academy Character Program (Gold Book). West Point: U.S. Military Academy, 2015.Accessed February 24, 2019. data.cape.army.mil/web/character-development-project/ repository/usma-character-development-strategy.pdf.

"Washington's Order Against Profanity." Ushistory.org. Accessed December 07, 2018. http://www.ushistory.org/valleyforge/ washington/profanity.html.

Wooden, John R., and Steve Jamison. *Wooden on Leadership*. New York: McGraw-Hill, 2005.

Zenger, Jack. "Are You Starting Too Late? A Head Start on the Path to Extraordinary." ZengerFolkman.com. 2014. Accessed February 24, 2019 http://zengerfolkman.com/wp-content/ uploads/2013/03/Leadership-Development-Are-You-Starting-Too-Late.pdf.

CATEGORY INDEX

INDEX

Made in the
USA
Columbia, SC